open

open

open

editorial

JORINDE SEIJDEL

THE RISE OF THE INFORMAL MEDIA

How Search Engines, Weblogs and
YouTube Change Public Opinion

The media through which news and
information are gathered, produced
and exchanged have expanded significantly over the last several years.
Weblogs, advanced search engines,
virtual environments like Second
Life, phenomena such as MySpace,
Hyves, Flickr and YouTube are offering new tools, communication options, social networks and platforms
for public debate. These are micro-
media or grassroots media: media
that are largely programmed, sup-
plied and broadcast by the user – in
contrast to conventional macromedia
such as television and the printed
press, which are more institutional-
ly determined. And these are 'informal media', used outside the formal
protocols and authorized precepts
of the old mass media, although, of
course, various overlaps exist.

The rise of the informal media
also implies the rise of the amateur, of the layperson or 'citizen
journalist' making public pro-
nouncements on all manner of social, cultural and political issues.
Andrew Keen, in *The Cult of the Amateur*
(2007), argues that the ascendance
of the masses is a threat to the
culture of authorities and experts,
with mediocrity becoming the norm.
He bemoans a lack of 'gatekeepers',
who can determine the value of news
and information on the internet. His
critique allows no room for considerations of the emancipating, democratizing or subversive effect of the
informal media.

Henry Jenkins, in his *Convergence
Culture: Where Old and New Media Collide*
(2006), is more nuanced about the
blurring of boundaries between media
producer and media user, between
the professional and the amateur – a
process he calls 'cultural convergence'. He emphasizes that this
process is born out of the interaction between the commercial media
industry and the user, out of nego-
tiations between the consumer and
the producer. The result is dynamic
and capricious, has no clear outcome
and is devoid of any set ideological
programme. According to Jenkins,
questions about the control of new
internet platforms are particularly
relevant.

In order not to be entirely lost
or carried away in today's public
sphere, in order to be a political,
social or cultural player, it seems
essential to study the new instruments and platforms that function
within that sphere critically. *Open*
13 features contributions by theorists and artists who reflect on the
implications of the informal media

for the public programme, conceived as the whole of public principles and requirements. Questions are raised about the conditions of our everyday media practices and about the opportunities for artists who work in a convergence culture.

Open 13 also includes specific attention to the changing position of conventional public media. Media scholar Oliver Marchart wonders how a radically democratic media policy can be conceived within the information society. The public dimension of television culture is also the focus of the special Hot Spot section compiled by Geert van de Wetering. Hot Spot, an initiative of the Dutch broadcasting organization VPRO, wants to investigate the implications and possibilities of the shifts in media production, distribution and consumption. How might programme makers benefit from an audience that participates in conceptualization and discussion?

Media philosopher Martijn de Waal assesses the democratic quotient of processes of valorization and systems of collective intelligence within the public sphere of Web 2.0. Internet critic Geert Lovink delves specifically on the expanding 'blogosphere'. He sees blogging as a nihilist enterprise that undermines traditional mass media without stepping forward as an alternative. Henry Jenkins' 'Nine Propositions Towards a Cultural Theory of YouTube' are included in the column. Media theorist Richard Grusin looks at the commotion around the Abu Ghraib photographs in light of our everyday media practices. Art theorist Willem van Weelden interviews web epistemologist Richard Rogers on the politics of information and the web as a discrete knowledge culture. Web sociologist Albert Benschop compares the 3-D structure of Second Life with the old, 'flat' web in relation to such aspects as methods of communication and the creation of power. DogTime students Arjan van Amsterdam and Sander Veenhof made a visual contribution. Artist and media researcher David Garcia sees, precisely within a commercial service industry in which media are omnipresent, opportunities for artists to contribute critical services and effective tools.

Artist Florian Göttke created a visual contribution derived from his project *Toppled*, an archive of news and amateur photographs taken from the internet, documenting the toppling of the statues of Saddam Hussein. I have written a text about iconoclasm and iconolatry and the potential of *Toppled* as a shadow archive. Felix Janssens and Kirsten Algera, of the design and communications agency TEAM TCHM and the makers of PRaudioGuide, produced the contribution *Hollow Model*, a number of templates with text in which they interrogate 'the public of the public' and the role that media and media use play in this. Is the public made hollow if it exists only in the media?

Oliver Marchart

The People and the Public

Radical Democracy and the Role of Public Media

According to political, cultural and media theorist Oliver Marchart, the degree to which public media are actually public depends on the political significance invested in the concept of democracy. He believes the main prerequisite for achieving a democratic media is the creation of an absolute democratic hegemony.

Part I: The Public and the Media

The focus of this essay is on one very simple question: how can a democratic – even a radically democratic – media policy be achieved, particularly with respect to public media?

In order to arrive at an answer – which can only be preliminary – to this question, we have to confront a whole range of questions regarding not only the nature of public media but also the nature of the state, of media policy, of politics and of democracy. Any attempt at answering this question has to start from an unstable and shifting terrain: To put it in the words of discourse analyst Jakob Torfing: 'The information society is not an established fact, but a terrain that is sustained and divided by social antagonisms and constantly reshaped by hegemonic struggles.'[1]

1. Jakob Torfing: *New Theories of Discourse: Laclau, Mouffe and Žižek* (Oxford/Malden: Blackwell, 1999), 211.

His statement has important consequences, for what it implies, in principle, is that the very terrain of the information society, if it is a hegemonic and thus political terrain, is open to change – and open to change not only for the worse, even if certain signs do point in that direction, but also the better. In other words, processes or developments within the information society do not unfold according to an iron logic or to irreversible laws (whether they be the laws of the market or the laws of what is presented as the only possible form of journalistic professionalism) that inevitably lead to a predictable outcome. Rather, the outcome of these processes is open because it is subjected to hegemonic struggle and, consequently, to progressive and emancipatory change.

Again, the supposedly iron laws of the market, while they may seem victorious at certain moments, do not proceed without encountering resistance from highly diverse forces – for example, the forces of alternative media and counter-media. All this takes place on a contested terrain, and what I want to sketch here – in a most preliminary fashion – are not only the contours of our status quo (concerning public media), which can be rather depressing at times, but also the emancipatory or radical democratic answers that can be used to address the status quo. This article, therefore, is divided in two parts. The first part, written from the viewpoint of political theory, is an overview of what I perceive to be the main obstacles to the development of a truly democratic public space in public media. This necessarily involves a reflection on the very nature of 'the public' or 'publicness' and the mass media, together with reflections on the nature of politics and of democracy. In the second part, I try to give a couple of answers or to at least suggest possible counter-strategies for a status quo that does not seem particularly conducive to a progressive or emancipatory redefinition of the role of public media. Admittedly, such counter-strategies imply, of necessity, a more informal usage of alternative media and counter-media.

Public Sphere

Let us begin with the simplest question. When talking about 'public broadcasting' or 'public media', what do we actually mean by 'public'? Why and, to put it differently, to what extent can public media reasonably be called 'public'? Common sense tells us that they are public because they constitute a public sphere. But can it be taken for granted that simply by virtue of being received by a mass public, by a mass audience, they do establish a public sphere and thus can be called 'public' media? On the other hand, if we derive the qualifier 'public' from the structure of their ownership, can it be taken for granted that simply by virtue of being owned publicly (that is to say, by virtue of being in public rather than in private hands) they can be called, and reasonably be called, 'public' media?

The answer to both questions is simply no. One of the last things so-called public media do nowadays is to actually constitute a public sphere. In a previous paper entitled 'Media Darkness',[2] which is a kind of prototype of the reflections presented here, I proposed a series of criteria or preconditions for the emergence of a truly public space. Let us look at the argument as developed there.

2. Oliver Marchart: 'Media Darkness: Reflections on Public Space, Light and Conflict', in: Tatiana Goryucheva and Eric Kluitenberg (eds.), *Media/Art/Public Domain* (Amsterdam: De Balie, Centre for Culture and Politics, 2003), 83-97; electronically available at http://www.debalie.nl/artikel.jsp?podiumid=media&articleid=19694.

Since Habermas, the first and most obvious criterion for publicness is accessibility. A space that is not accessible – physically or otherwise – is not a public space. It is a space of exclusion and, in this sense, a private space. Only if, potentially, everybody can gain access to a certain space can this space be called 'public' in the strict sense. One barely has to mention the fact that most so-called public media do not meet this criterion of accessibility – not only because they are inaccessible physically (since public space in the strict sense is not a physical

space) but also because they do not allow for voices other than the usual ones to be made public. Only the dominant or hegemonic discourses are allowed access. I will return to the question of hegemony later, but let me just say that nothing is more misleading than the common-sensical notion of freedom of opinion as long as there are no media through which opinions can be transmitted. In a liberal democracy we may own the right to have our own opinions, but if these opinions cannot be heard publicly, what are we to do with them? Carry them within our hearts, as personal secrets? Even under authoritarian conditions of tyranny or despotism, it is perfectly possible to be granted the right to have private opinions – as long as we do not express them publicly. If democracy differs from authoritarianism, as the definitions suggest, it is precisely because those in a democracy have not only the right to hold personal opinions but also the actual opportunity to voice them publicly, that is to say, to have a voice that can be heard and made heard, and a position that can be seen and made seen. Therefore, the typically liberal minimal definition of rights, currently hegemonic, does not get us very far. Also needed are the material conditions that enable us to make our voices heard and our political positions seen: public media should be precisely these means or material conditions, and public space should be precisely the stage on which our political opinions can appear and be seen by everybody. Thus mere accessibility is followed by a second requirement: the criterion of visibility. 'Public visibility' describes a condition: the existence of a space in which one's voice can be heard and one's political position – one's public opinion as opposed to a 'merely private' opinion – can be perceived.

A Space of Conflict

The need for public visibility is followed immediately by a third condition, for a space in which the most diverse political opinions and standpoints are staged is, inevitably, a space of conflict. To discuss public space in a meaningful way is to discuss 'conflictuality'. Only a space in which a single opinion exists can be a space without conflict. As soon as diverse and incompatible opinions appear, they enter into a conflictive relationship. Again, if we look at public broadcasting, we never encounter a real conflict; what we encounter is the simulacrum of conflict. This has to do with the formatting of TV or radio debates, but on a more fundamental level it also has to do with the role and function of public media as machines or apparatuses for the production and reproduction of a given hegemony. As Stuart Hall, among others, has shown, public media have to present themselves in the mode of 'objectivity', which is another name for consensus. Of course, objectivity is a fiction, but it is the fiction public media have to produce on a daily basis in order to legitimate themselves, as well as to legitimate the dominant hegemonic formation (the 'way things are' here, in our corner of the world). In cases of social conflict, public media thus have to take a seemingly objective or neutral stance vis-à-vis all conflicting parties. They have to search for a consensual position, and if it cannot be found, they have to produce one.[3]

In order to understand the role of public media, it is absolutely imperative to investigate how public consent and consensus are established – or fail to be established on certain occasions. The name for the establishment of consensus and consent, since Gramsci, is 'hegemony'. Hegemony is the ideological cement, as it were, that binds the ruling classes together in a hegemonic block. The material of which such cement consists is dis-

3. Let us take the infamous example of reports on German television, public and private, concerning Schröder's so-called social reforms. To call these policies – which are not only a German phenomenon, of course – 'reforms' is, as we all know, a euphemistic way to speak about the dismantling and thorough destruction of the welfare state. In political talk shows on German TV, you will not find a single topic rehearsed more frequently than these reforms. Obviously, German television has to rehearse the topic in a seemingly objective and neutral fashion. But what does this mean in practice? If you analyse a talk show like that of Sabine Christiansen, where the so-called reforms were discussed on a nearly weekly basis, initially you see that the pros and cons are given space, and that guests both defend and attack the reforms. A closer look, however, immediately reveals the presence of significantly more defenders than opponents of these reforms (in most cases, not one opponent even questions their necessity). If, for instance, six politicians or experts have been invited to debate the issues, at least five of them adhere to the hegemonic discourse or *doxa*, which basically says that one may disagree about the speed and scope of the so-called reforms but not about the urgent need to reform (read: to slowly but steadily dismantle) the welfare state. In order to go on constructing the fiction of objectivity, a single guest, most often a member of a labour union, presents a slightly different view. In most cases, however, he or she still subscribes to the assumed necessity for reforms. At no point in the discourse is the dominant hegemonic horizon that forms the backdrop of the debate put into question. This is somewhat surprising, because as these debates are taking place the discourse on the supposed urgency and inevitability of reforms has been promoted – and partly put into policies – for about 20 years. Nearly the entire published opinion of all mainstream media – electronic as well as print media – agrees on this point, and yet the people – more on 'the people' in a moment – stubbornly disagree. All opinion polls show that the people are less than convinced of the supposed necessity of robbing them of all the achievements of the welfare state. Although every conflict concerning this question has been effectively banned from the public media, it remains impossible for the dominant hegemony to establish a consensus *outside* the media and publicized opinion. As far as I can see, no political topic exists in which publicized opinion differs more significantly from common sense, or the opinion in the street.

course. It is in and through discourse that hegemony is established, and the most important machines or apparatuses that construct and reproduce hegemony are the media. And the more those media appear to be objective and neutral, the better they can do their job of constructing and reproducing consensus.[4]

4. This point has been made by Stuart Hall in his article: 'The rediscovery of "ideology": return of the repressed in media studies', in Michael Gurevitch, Tony Bennett, James Curran and Janet Wollacott (eds.), *Culture, Society and the Media* (London: Routledge, 1982).

Herein we might encounter the main reason why the aforementioned criteria and conditions for publicness are seldom met by so-called public media. Were they to be implemented, they would certainly threaten the role and function of these hegemony machines and, thus, of the dominant hegemonic formation. This is the reason why conflict and antagonism are not allowed to reappear within public media. Why does the state not open up public media in terms of accessibility and conflict? Why are public media not simply turned into public places in the strict sense? The questions may sound naive, but the answers, I hope, are not. In the moment of conflict – if conflict is allowed to enter public media, thus making them truly public – the state immediately encounters the danger of state media turning into counter-media. By allowing conflict and antagonism to unfold, an open-ended play is set in motion whose outcome remains undecided. This is precisely what the political is about. As soon as a truly political process unfolds around a certain conflict, you cannot determine in advance what the outcome will be and which side will be the winner. This is the reason why state media have to

produce consent and not conflict: because the political in the strict sense – conflict – must not surface. It has to be kept at bay, neutralized by the impression of consensus and objectivity. For the same reason, the role and function of public media are to depoliticize the political. Whenever conflict – a strike, a demonstration, an uproar, a revolt – appears, public media have to give official, consensual and 'objective' meaning to it; and if such meaning is not readily available, they have to construct it.

Antagonism

A review of the first part of the essay shows that accessibility, visibility and conflict are necessary criteria or preconditions for the emergence of public space, and it is possible, of course, to find additional criteria. At this point I want to claim that all imaginable criteria, including accessibility and visibility, are in fact secondary to the necessity for conflict. Unlike those Habermasian liberals who think the definitive criterion for publicness is rationality – expressed in the form of undisturbed rational deliberation – I am claiming that it is not rationality but conflict and that public space in the strict sense emerges wherever a conflict breaks out. The implication is that public space does not have a definite place, and that public media are far from being such a location. Rather, conflict looks for and creates its own location, which can be anywhere. For this admittedly rather strong notion of conflict, I have borrowed a term used by Laclau and Mouffe: antagonism.[5] The

5. Ernesto Laclau and Chantal Mouffe: *Hegemony and Socialist Strategy* (London/New York: Verso, 1985).

priority of antagonism over other criteria, such as accessibility and visibility, becomes quite evident when one observes that when real social conflict breaks out, people link up with one side or the other, thus widening the space in which such conflict appears. Take revolution, for example, certainly the most dramatic and radical form of social antagonism. A revolution takes place in public or rather creates a public of its own, along with newly accessible public space in which people can participate. The streets, formerly an urban space reserved for traffic, are transformed into a political stage: a public space in the strict sense. Simultaneously, opinions formerly suppressed may become visible; voices formerly silenced may become heard. But in a stronger sense, something more fundamental becomes visible: the fact that things can be changed, that consensus can vanish and that consent can disappear. In other words, it becomes apparent that no hegemonic formation is eternal and that every hegemonic formation constitutes, in the manner of the 'information society', 'a terrain that is sustained and divided by social antagonisms and constantly reshaped by hegemonic struggles'.

This awareness leads to important conclusions with respect to our understanding of public media and all things related to public media. If true publicness emerges in the presence of antagonism – and only in the presence of antagonism – it follows that media can be called 'public' only when they allow for the emergence of conflict within their institutional structure. Wouldn't truly democratic media have to allow for the possibility of contestation, for the possibility of putting into question the established consensus? Isn't democracy – contrary to what Habermas may think – simply unperceivable without the possibility of conflict and antagonism? If the answer is yes, how do we envisage democratic public media? And, an even more pressing question, how can we invent strategies to democratize the media?

Part II: The People and Radical Democracy

The picture I've painted is not as bleak as it may seem at first glance, precisely because hegemony is always a contested terrain and because no hegemonic block is in total control of popular consent. For the same reason, there are always strategies available for undermining hegemonic consensus and creating some form of counter-hegemony. What I would like to propose are a couple of strategies for creating counter-public spaces within and outside so-called public media. Yet, as I see it, it is absolutely necessary to proceed from the correct starting point, politically speaking, for if these strategies are to be in the least bit successful and to have some sort of political effect, they have to be located within the democratic hypothesis. They have to be democratic, or rather radically democratic. We get nowhere by clinging to an obsolete idea of a completely different political position – revolutionary, pseudo-communist or whatever – outside the democratic realm established by the French Revolution. Emancipatory strategies today, if they are to be successful, have to expand, deepen and perhaps radicalize the democratic realm, but not dismantle or depart from it altogether (as theorists like Slavoj Žižek, for instance, are currently proposing from a sort of neo-Leninist stance). This does not mean that we have to submit to the hegemonic consensus of existing liberal-democratic regimes. Instead, we have to counter the minimal definition of democracy – as a minimal institutional framework that includes a free-market economy – with a maximal definition and a project aimed at radical democracy.

Before describing a radical democratic media policy and the role of public media in a project aimed at radical democracy, I want to point out that a genuine radicalization of the democratic realm requires, in a sense, a reinstatement of the democratic sovereign. That is to say, we have to put the question of popular sovereignty back on the agenda, because this is what democracy is all about. To put it bluntly, we have to talk about the role of 'the people' in democracy – in much the same way that we have to put 'the people' between quotation marks – because their role has no substance or essence prior to democracy's construction. As we cannot dwell on the consequences of this act for political theory, let me simply state the consequences for media theory. One quite revealing fact is that the etymological roots of the term 'public' are systematically neglected. Where does the meaning of the Latin adjective *publicus* – the source of all English terms derived from that root, such as 'public space', 'the public' or even 'publicity' – come from? The answer is that *publicus* derives from *populus*, Latin for 'the people'. We have become wholly oblivious to the original connection between 'the public' and 'the people'. In thinking of public media today, we

have completely lost sight of 'the people', except as a phantasmal entity: a mere number to be counted in the form of audience ratings.

This is the pseudo-democracy of the market, where we encounter not 'the people' but 'the consumer'. And the field in which consumers operate is not the public, in the political sense of the term, but publicity. Within a dominant hegemony, 'the people' is redefined as a market subject. We encounter this development throughout society, but, most devastatingly, it spills back from the market into the political field proper, where suddenly the subject of politics is redefined as the market subject of the consumer who is free to make a choice among various products (political parties, for example) which ultimately turn out to be nearly identical. Thus we are left with a choice that makes no difference – an entirely apolitical choice – as politics begins, and begins precisely, where a decision is taken which in actual fact *does* make a difference. The media discourse on audience ratings is perfectly compatible if not complicit with this larger hegemonic process of redefining what counts as the sovereign in democracy, which is 'the people', along with the basic options available to the people for actualizing this state of sovereignty. As soon as we are left with a choice that makes no real difference, we are left with no choice at all, and thus without the capacity to act either politically or publicly.

Media of the People

If it is correct that our current idea of the public – in the sense of publicity – does not include the people (except in terms of audience ratings and, perhaps, talk shows), we have arrived, conversely, at a positive feature – or, if you wish, a positive principle or slogan – of a radical democratic media policy: 'public' derives from 'the people', thus public media must be the media of the people, not the media of the state or the ruling block.

But what does this mean in practice? Obviously, the last thing we want to do is to give a *völkisch* meaning to 'the people'. Hence, 'the people' is not a substance in the ethnic sense. This would be the totalitarian meaning of 'the people', and obviously we do not need an ethnicized form of publicness. The democratic conception of 'the people' is entirely different, because it does not assume that 'the people' is a predetermined body capable of being found in empirical reality. (Nor is 'the public' a predetermined body.) In democracy, 'the people' is de-substantialized and remains present only in two forms, both of which are highly important for a radical democratic project. The first form or meaning in which 'the people' remains present in democracy is the citizen, which evokes an image of market squares in ancient civilizations, where citizens gathered, freely and equally, to debate public affairs. The second meaning to be kept in mind is the social meaning of 'the people' as the underclass – as those excluded from the public domain. In the 19th century, from a socialist standpoint, this part of the population was perceived mainly as the working classes. Today we know that many more groups are excluded from public, political and social participation, such as the jobless, immigrants and *sans papiers*. 'The people', in the sense of the

excluded, refers to those who are reduced to silence, who have no voice. A public space that does not grant accessibility and visibility to these groups is not a public space in any meaningful sense. Therefore, an understanding of public space as a space for 'the people' and of 'the people' has to be reinvigorated, or reinvented. A radical democratic project must seek to establish a counter-hegemony around a notion of 'the people' as both the citizens and the excluded, while the dominant hegemony defining 'the people' as the consumers, or as a nationalist or ethnic entity, has to be confronted.

Public media can be made public only if we engage in a hegemonic struggle as described here. It is not enough to have a good media policy; we need a good political policy. In other words, public media can be transformed into public spaces only when the transformation is part of a larger political project encompassing other political fields, such as social policies, economic policies, educational policies and so forth. Any effort made to democratize the media must take part within a larger effort to democratize society; otherwise it will not be successful.

Democratic Counter-Hegemony

But how to construct such a radical democratic counter-hegemony? Obviously, this is a difficult and protracted process which would have to take place on a multiplicity of levels and within a multiplicity of social fields. It would have to include the democratization of schools and other educational institutions, as well as the democratization of the workplace. And it would include, of course, the democratization of the media. In order to implement this process, we must confront the dominant hegemonic block at its ideological level: that is, at the level of consensus. It is at this level that a political or hegemonic struggle rages over the question as to what counts and does not count as legitimate in society. One has to confront the dominant hegemonic block on this legitimatory ground – on the field of legitimation – and to redefine what counts as legitimate policy. Involved in this type of confrontation is a struggle over concepts and words. Take the notion of efficiency. Today, previous democratic achievements are being demolished throughout society in the name of economic efficiency. Universities, for instance, which had already been democratized in the '70s to some degree, are being handed over to the market and to the imperative of economic efficiency. A counter-hegemonic struggle would not necessarily deny the need for an 'efficient' policy, but it would transform the meaning of the term; it would change what counts as efficient. Why not count as efficient those policies that deepen and radicalize democracy by increasing, for instance, accessibility to certain institutions? Such a move would re-legitimate or re-define the criteria by which state subsidies are allocated to certain institutions. Then, only those institutions that work efficiently in the sense of fostering and deepening democratic participation could legitimately claim state money. This is a particularly important argument with respect to cultural policies, an area in which the role of many independent cultural institutions is constantly threatened and in need of self-legitimation if these institutions are to be subsidized. If demo-

cratic efficiency were to be made a general principle of cultural policy, state subsidies would no longer be fed into the entertainment industry, for instance, or into representational forms of bourgeois culture, but only into those institutions which in actual fact contribute to the creation of a democratic public.

Now let us apply the same idea to public media. How is their privileged role (vis-à-vis private media) usually legitimized? A good example is that of Austrian public broadcaster ORF (in political reality, it is state TV). According to Austria's public-broadcasting law, ORF's special status is legitimized by the law's informational, cultural and educational mission. Although private media cannot be forced to implement a decent informational or cultural policy, the law requires public TV to do so. A closer look, however, shows that Austrian law prescribes such a general humanistic policy not only with respect to the informational, cultural and educational mission of public broadcasting. The law also says that ORF should provide decent entertainment and – at this point it becomes rather absurd – that public television should motivate people to engage in sports. This is to be achieved both by covering sports events and by including as many other sports-related programmes as possible – in order to reach those parts of the audience that do not regularly watch sports coverage. By referring to the need to improve the *Volksgesundheit*, the law explicitly calls for the indoctrination of the populace. Here, again, we encounter 'the people' in the ethnic or *völkisch* sense of the term, as an object of biopolitical regulation. Surely it is more than obvious that, from a radical democratic point of view, public broadcasting should not be an instrument of biopolitical indoctrination. But a law that requires public media to provide entertainment is already intrinsically undemocratic. I have nothing against entertainment as such, but I have strong objections to a state that prescribes public entertainment by law. This seems to be premised on the rather awkward idea that people do not know how to entertain themselves and need the state and its public institutions to entertain them. We are reminded of 'rule by entertainment' or the old Roman *panem et circenses*. This is not the republican Rome of the forum, however, but rather the Rome of despotism, in which the forum is replaced by the circus – and public space is turned into an arena for entertainment. To re-democratize public media implies prescribing a different task for them: as public media, they would have to provide the institutional conditions necessary for 'the people' to gain access to a public audience and to make their voices heard in public. They would have to provide for spaces of inclusion rather than exclusion, and they would have to provide platforms for citizens to assemble and debate – to enter into conflict on – the most diverse matters of public interest. This can succeed only if such spaces or platforms are turned over to 'the people'-as-producers (in the sense in which Walter Benjamin speaks about the artist as producer), also on an institutional level, which would lead to the development of media platforms with forms of self-management that ruled out the need for control by either the state or political parties. Consequently, public media would assume the role and status of alternative media.

Distribution of Public Funds

Although my proposals may sound rather utopian, they are not, as this radical democratic programme does not have to be implemented full scale. Of course, if it were to be implemented full scale, it would amount to the total destruction (and subsequent reconstruction) of public broadcasting as we know it. But I do not envision the state's main TV station handing over all Saturday evening primetime slots to 'the people'. Far more realistic is to force public media, by law, to open and hand over parts of their means of production to the wider public, thus allowing for the creation of democratic media platforms. In addition, if the main legitimatory goal of public policies is to democratize as many social areas as possible, including public media, a logical result is the reallocation of public funds. Currently, public broadcasting in many European countries is subsidized by audience fees. Now, if for some reason public media will not relinquish access to their radio or television frequencies and to their means of production – the most likely situation in the near future – part of the money derived from audience fees will have to go to those media within civil society which in actual fact do provide the institutional framework necessary for public spaces to emerge. These fees will have to be reallocated to alternative and democratic media institutions.

All such measures and media policies, and one can imagine many more, are in fact premised on a change in political hegemony. Hence they involve a larger and no doubt protracted process of politicization/democratization of society in which the democratization of the media will play a particular and perhaps central part, but certainly not the only part. It is necessary to modify the consensus of opinion regarding what counts as legitimate. As long as the (symbolic) majority thinks it is legitimate for taxpayers' money to go into public institutions if, and only if, such institutions succumb to the imperative of economic efficiency, the task of democratizing them will be immensely difficult. For this reason, the hegemonic struggle does not start within these institutions (in order to reform them from within). It starts within the minds of the people. This is why a new democratic consensus, a new democratic hegemony, has to be established.

In conclusion, eight essential points:

1. In terms of legitimacy, public media can be called public only to the extent that they are accessible to 'the people' and allow a space of conflict to emerge.

2. Only those media that are truly public, as defined in Point 1, can be called democratic.

3. Given these criteria, public media as we know them – that is to say, public media within our existing liberal-democratic regimes – are neither public nor democratic.

4. It follows that, from a democratic point of view, public media have to be 'made public' through a process of democratization.

5. In order to democratize the media, we have to democratize democracy; in other words, we have to radicalize and deepen the democratic realm. We can call this project 'radical democracy'.

6. The democratization of the media is a cornerstone of any radical democratic programme, because democracy occurs only where there is public space; and, among other places in society, public media have the material and institutional infrastructure to provide the conditions for public space to emerge.

7. The democratization of public media can succeed only if this process is part of a larger hegemonic struggle. The radicalization of democracy at all levels involves both a change in the way people envisage their lives within society and the construction of a new counter-hegemonic consensus.

8. Last but not least, the struggle for truly democratic public media is not a question of media policy. If we leave it to technocrats, bureaucrats or media consultants to invent new media policies, nothing will change. For radical democracy is not about inventing a new policy but about inventing new politics – and inventing politics anew.

Toppled

Visual Contribution
by Florian Göttke

Artist Florian Göttke has
contributed a submission on
his *Toppled* project, created
especially for *Open* 13, in
collaboration with German graphic
designer Felix Weigand. Its
pages are distributed throughout
the issue. Jorinde Seijdel's
explanatory text about the work
can be found on page 146.

Martijn de Waal

From Media Landscape to Media Ecology

The Cultural Implications of Web 2.0

In this essay, media philosopher Martijn de Waal examines the implications of the rise of Web 2.0 for the public sphere and its democratic content. Who decides what is of value in the new media ecosystem and how do important processes take place?

Over twelve months ago, the Francophone press in Belgium filed a lawsuit against Google News. The papers wanted to prevent their news reports from automatically appearing on Google's web pages. The issue at stake was this: should 'news aggregators' – 'News 2.0 services' in the buzzword lingo of internet watchers – be allowed simply to pluck headlines from newspapers, weblogs and other news providers and then rearrange them on their own sites using an often secret algorithm? This is not just a copyright issue. Equally important is the corresponding cultural debate as to who should be in charge of bringing order to the media landscape. Who is to control the public sphere? Who is to determine what is of value in it? Is this the preserve of experts and professionals like journalists? Or would it actually be more democratic to leave the process to Google's computer algorithms and Wikipedia's egalitarian peer-to-peer networks?

With the rise of Web 2.0[1] the traditional gatekeepers of the public sphere are facing competition from new players. On the one hand there is the 'collective intelligence' of 'aggregators' like Google News, Nujij.nl, Digg and Newsvine. On the other hand, the position of traditional experts is being undermined by 'collaborative intelligence' systems such as Wikipedia in which media users cooperate in an egalitarian manner. What do these developments mean for the public sphere and for processes of

1. A term encapsulating a concept of the internet as a huge database of content, to which anyone can contribute data and in which the data can be linked in a wide variety of ways. This is in contrast to Web 1.0, which consisted of static web pages.

'valorization'? What is the precise role of technology in these processes? Is this – as Web 2.0 gurus and entrepreneurs frequently maintain – really a question of democratization? Are we entering the era of smart mobs, adhocracies and issue politics?

From a Media Landscape to a Media Ecology

The basic premise of this discussion is that the hierarchical and centralist architecture of the media landscape is turning into a more decentralized peer-to-peer network, a media 'ecosystem'. That being so, it is time to refine the linear flow chart of the media landscape usually found in media and communications studies handbooks with a dash of chaos theory. Traditionally, the media production process is depicted as a chain in which the individual links are connected by arrows pointing to the right. Media 'content' (or, more broadly, cultural product) is produced in institutional environments after which this content is 'packaged' (for example, by broadcasters and publishers), then distributed, and finally consumed.

Insights derived from cultural studies have taught us that in each segment of this chain, 'encoding' and 'decoding' processes take place. The encoding processes on the left-hand side of the chain have their origins in institutional contexts with their associated professional codes and cultures, or are prompted by economic considerations like shareholder profit maximization or ideological motives. On the right-hand side of the chain, the decoding process takes place from the perspective of specific cultural identities. Based on their experience, the public invests the message with meaning, while at the same time those meanings help to form their experiences of identities.

Developments in the media landscape have changed this process in at least two important ways. Firstly, the scarcity in this system has decreased, thanks to increasing access to cheap production methods and distribution networks, resulting in an extra link in the chain immediately prior to consumption: the 'filter'. In the scarcity system, the supply is determined by the gatekeepers, who work for the 'packagers'. In a system without scarcity, the supply is more or less unlimited, but a filter mechanism (search machine, portal, Amazon algorithm, the long tail, social networks, collective intelligence) matches supply to the demand of the media consumer.

Some of these filters are devised by institutional organizations (commercial publishers, public broadcasters) with interests of their own. Others are the result of feedback data from media usage. Every book ordered from Amazon has an impact on the lists of 'personal recommendations' presented to subsequent buyers. And every link from a blog to an article in a newspaper raises that paper's 'page ranking' in Google and thus its visibility and potential authority. This process is also known as 'collective intelligence'.

The second change concerns the process of decoding, at the far right of the chain. In the traditional media model that process was chiefly confined to the private or parochial sphere; now it has become part of the media chain – and the public sphere – both directly and indirectly. Directly, because all manner of interpretations and 'remixes' of commentary on media products are now part of the media landscape via blogs or Youtube. In *Convergence Culture*, Henry Jenkins explains how the roles of cultural producer and cultural consumer are steadily converging. He even alludes to the emergence of a new 'folk culture', a cultural system in which narratives have no definitive form but are continually being retold.[2] Encoding becomes in effect a process of 'recoding' that produces new content, which can in turn be 'packaged', filtered and consumed. This process could also be called 'collaborative intelligence'.

2. Henry Jenkins, *Convergence Culture* (New York: New York University Press, 2006). See also the theories of Lawrence Lessig in which he explains how nearly all cultural manifestations and innovative ideas are in fact a 'remix' of earlier cultural manifestations.

All of which means that it would be more accurate to talk about a media ecology than a media landscape. Whereas a landscape is a metaphor that conjures up a static image, ecology does justice to the notion of a system that is in a state of flux.

Traditional Authorities Versus 'Those People in Pyjamas'

How and where in such a media ecology is it decided what is of value, which cultural products 'matter'? In systems of collaborative intelligence, users work together on the basis of equality to create meaning and compile knowledge. Wikipedia and open source software like Linux are perhaps the best-known examples of such systems. Charles Leadbeater has dubbed this phenomenon 'We-think'. 'In the We-Think economy people don't just want services and goods delivered to them. They also want tools so that they can take part and places in which to play, share, debate with others.'[3] There is a caveat to this, of course. Such a system only works as long as the participants

3. http://www.wethink-thebook.net/ (accessed 13 June 2007).

trust one another, accept one another's knowledge, or at any rate are prepared to discuss it. Because whose opinion counts when there are conflicting views?

It is no accident that most of these systems are subject to new forms of institutionalization of expertise and reliability.[4] The best-known examples are reputation systems like the ones that operate on online marketplaces like Ebay. Then there are the 'Karma' rating systems such as introduced on the Slashdot website. Writers and commentators can earn karma points by contributing to the community. Contributions from visitors are also rated and visitors can in turn filter contributions according to their rating.

4. The website Edge.org recently hosted an extensive discussion about the role of experts in systems of collaborative intelligence. Wikipedia founder Larry Sanger explained that he eventually came to regard Wikipedia's egalitarian knowledge paradigm as counterproductive and accordingly set up an alternative – the Citizendium – where validation is once again carried out by experts. See: Larry Sanger, 'Who Says we Know. On the New Politics of Knowledge' on Edge.org, http://www.edge.org/3rd_culture/sanger07/sanger07_index.html.

The expert paradigm in which experts accredited by official bodies determine what is true and what not, is being replaced here by a more meritocratic system where what counts is proven expertise rather than institutional embeddedness. A new balance will grad-

ually emerge, and new collective forms of canonization. In a recent discussion on Edge.org about authority on Wikipedia (quoted by Henk Blanken on the *Nieuwe Reporter* blog), Gloria Origgi wrote: 'An efficient knowledge system like Wikipedia inevitably will grow by generating a variety of evaluative tools: that is how culture grows, how traditions are created. What is a cultural tradition? A labelling system of insiders and outsiders, of who stays on and who is lost in the magma of the past. The good news is that in the Web era this inevitable evaluation is made through new, collective tools that challenge the received views and develop and improve an innovative and democratic way of selection of knowledge. But there's no escape from the creation of a "canonical" – even if tentative and rapidly evolving – corpus of knowledge.'[5]

5. Henk Blanken, 'Deugen journalisten? (On Sanger's Citizendium)', in: *De Nieuwe Reporter*, 21.5.2007. http://www.denieuwereporter.nl/?p=963 (accessed 5 June 2007).

This is not to say that the role of traditional gatekeepers and the mass media is played out. The various systems of 'peer-to-peer co-production' that are emerging in different places are not isolated but linked to one another in a layered model. Henry Jenkins foresees the emergence of a model in which the traditional mass media and the new niche or amateur media enjoy a symbiotic relationship. The mainstream media still manage to reach large groups in society and continue to exert considerable influence on the public debate. They provide for shared cultural frameworks, they establish cultural symbols. A great deal of cultural production occurs bottom-up in the 'grassroots media' which by definition focus on a small group of fans or conversely, critical users. Those grassroots media can also act as a control mechanism on the mass media. If the mainstream media abuse their authority, this can be raised in the niche media.[6]

But at the end of the day, such criticism still needs to be validated by the mainstream media. Bloggers may keep a critical watch on CBS news broadcasts and discover that a negative story about George Bush's National Service record is based on forged documents, but anchorman Dan Rather only stands down when the *New York Times* picks up the report and in so doing validates it. 'Those people in pyjamas', as a CBS senior executive initially described the bloggers, thereby implying that their allegations are not to be taken seriously because they don't belong to the professional media, are perfectly capable of bringing matters to the attention of the public. But when it comes to validation, the mainstream media are for the time being indispensable. 'Broadcasting provides the common culture, and the Web offers more localized channels for responding to that culture,' according to Jenkins.[7]

A more layered model than Jenkins' dichotomy between mass media and niche media can be found in Yochai Benkler's *The Wealth of Networks*, in which he explains how, in the media ecology of the internet, the production, distribution and valorisation of ideas and meaning proceeds via a complex and graduated process. A small number of sites attract a large public, he states, while the vast majority of sites appeal to a very limited public. Discussions between peers may well take place on such niche sites, but many of those niche websites are in turn monitored by sites that appeal to a wider public, the so-called 'A-list bloggers'. When they flag something interesting on a niche site this triggers a sudden flurry of visits to the site in question. That high level of interest may ebb away after a while, but it's not unknown for a niche site to evolve into a new authority. Benkler: 'Filtering, accreditation, synthesis and salience are created through a system of peer review by information affinity groups, topical or interest based. These groups filter the observations and opinions of an enormous range of people and transmit those that pass local peer review to broader groups and ultimately to the polity more broadly without recourse to market-based point of control over the information flow.'[8]

Alongside this layered system of various forms of peer production, processes of 'valorisation' also take place in systems of 'collective intelligence'. Collective intelligence is not the result of deliberate collaboration, but is a by-product of other processes – in systems theory it is known as 'emergence'. In a discussion on Edge.org, Benkler describes how it works: 'Take Google's algorithm. It aggregates the distributed

6. For the time being it appears that bloggers only monitor certain kinds of news reports. In the USA it is primarily politically charged news that is put under the microscope. The number of known cases in which 'fraudulent' reporting of other topics has been exposed by bloggers is considerably smaller. See: Maarten Reijnders 'Journalistieke fraude en de rol van het publiek' in: *De Nieuwe Reporter* http://www.denieuwereporter.nl/?p=553 (accessed 14 June 2007).

7. Jenkins, *Convergence Culture*, op. cit. (note 2), 211.

8. Yochai Benkler, *The Wealth of Networks* (New Haven: Yale University Press, 2006), 246.

judgments of millions of people who have bothered to host a webpage. It doesn't take any judgment, only those that people care enough about to exert effort to insert a link in their own page to some other page. . . . It doesn't ask the individuals to submerge their identity, or preferences, or actions in any collective effort. No one spends their evenings in consensus-building meetings. It merely produces a snapshot of how they spend their scarce resources: time, web-page space, expectations about their readers' attention. That is what any effort to synthesize a market price does.'[9]

9. Yochai Benkler, 'On "Digital Maoism: The Hazards of the New Online Collectivism" By Jaron Lanier', Edge.org, 2006, http://www.edge.org/discourse/digital_maoism.html (accessed 5 June 2007).

The use of social bookmark systems like Del.icio.us, media-use analysis software such as can be found at Last.fm, or the kind of Long-tail implementations offered by Amazon.com, work in a similar way. In *Pop-up*, authors Henk Blanken and Mark Deuze call this the 'metacracy': 'The metacracy is what you get when mathematical algorithms elevate the wisdom of the masses to the norm. . . . The power of the media shifts to the faceless masses. New "social software" will compile the news for us the way we want it, before we even knew that was how we wanted it. The successors of Digg and Google will know our preferences, our weaknesses and our passions and put together a media menu that satisfies our taste and expectations.'[10] Authority develops in the process of what has been called 'collaborative filtering': an aggregated analysis of the activity of every node in the net-

10. Henk Blanken and Mark Deuze, *Pop-up* (Amsterdam: Boom, 2007).

work. Just as the 'invisible hand' of the market economy determines the 'right' price for every product, so the 'collective intelligence' spawned by a combination of social networks and computer algorithms determines which articles or programmes are worthwhile, or pressing or important.

How Intelligent is 'Collective Intelligence'?

Such developments are often presented as democratic. Thanks to these systems, it is claimed, we are on the one hand able to compile the knowledge scattered across the network (rather than having to depend on the accredited knowledge of a social elite), and on the other hand we have greater freedom when it comes to making choices within the media ecology. In this we are assisted by smart software that points us in the direction of the sorts of things that might interest us, or that these collective systems have decided are important. 'The metacracy has obvious advantages,' argue Blanken and Deuze. 'It is an open system in which everyone can see what we collectively think, what the trends are, the signs of the times, and what is important.'[11] And according to Leadbeater 'the dominant ethos of We-Think economy is democratic and egalitarian'.[12] In many of these discourses the mass media are contrastingly portrayed as aristocratic and paternalistic bastions that have completely lost touch with what people are really thinking. Typical is this quote from *Wikinomics* by Don Tap-

11. Ibid.

12. http://www.wethinkthebook.net/ (accessed 13 June 2007).

scott and Anthony Williams: 'Regardless of their differences both sites [Slashdot and Digg] make most traditional news outlets look like archaic relics of a bygone era.' To add weight to their argument, the authors go on to cite the founder of News 2.0 website Rabble.ca Judy Rebick: 'The mainstream media people define themselves as the arbiters of taste. . . . As long as the media think they know what's right, she continues, they'll never be in a position to harness people's collective intelligence.'[13]

13. Don Tapscott and Anthony Williams, *Wikinomics: How Mass Collaboration Changes Everything* (London: Penguin Books, 2006).

Nonetheless, this putative democratization, or at any rate its positive implications for the public sphere, has its critics. In the first place, the feedback mechanisms in the media ecosystem can also result in collective folly or media hypes, as Steven Johnson has shown in *Emergence*. Johnson describes how, in the early 1990s, the Gennifer Flowers affair became a media hype despite the fact that the editors of the major American television news bulletins – the traditional gatekeepers in this media landscape – had originally decided not to devote any air time to the matter. The private life of a politician was not news, was the initial judgement. But they had reckoned without an important change that had recently taken place in the media landscape. Until the mid 1980s, the national networks delivered a series of selected, ready-to-air news items to affiliated local broadcasters. But around that time, local television stations acquired access to CNN's video databases containing all the uncut and unused material. Whereas previously it had been New York that decided what the local stations could broadcast, now they could make their own pick – a decentralization of authorization within the network. Many local stations accordingly decided to run the news about the Flowers case. The following day all the national newscasts opened with the item – after the news had done the rounds at the local level, they could no longer ignore it.[14]

14. Steven Johnson, *Emergence* (New York: Scribner, 2002).

Geert Lovink has described a similar process. On blogs, the use of 'snarky' language (a 'cynical mannerism') provokes a lot of fuss, and thus a lot of incoming links, and thus a higher 'page rank'. In other words, the blog culture, rather than producing intelligent debates, leads to point-scoring contests and invective. This was also one of the reasons why David Winer gave up blogging: 'I don't enjoy being the go-to guy for snarky folk who try to improve their page-rank by idiotic tirades about their supposed insights into my character.'[15] So while the way filters work is determined by media use and processes

15. See also Geert Lovink, 'Blogging, the Nihilist Impulse' in *Zero Comments, Blogging and Critical Internet Culture* (New York: Routledge, 2007).

of decoding, conversely this mechanism influences the process of encoding. An arresting headline on the front page of a newspaper is not the same as an easily found headline in Google, as journalists are nowadays well aware, having meanwhile attended one of the countless courses in search engine optimization. Anyone who aspires to be heard in the media ecosystem will need to adjust their language to the patented and secret rules of the search engine.

Some critics fear that processes of collective and collaborative intelligence are leading to cultural trivialization. Collaborative intelligence leads to bland compromises, collective intelligence to populism and even to tunnel vision. That may be democratic, but it is not good for society or for the quality of cultural production, say the critics. One of them, Andrew Keen, even regards the democratization that occurs in the media ecology as downright undesirable: 'As Adorno liked to remind us, we have a responsibility to protect people from their worst impulses. If people aren't able to censor their worst instincts, then they need to be censored by others wiser and more disciplined than themselves.'[16] And that wiser entity is not a search engine or Web 2.0, but the cultural pope. 'Without an elite mainstream media, we will lose our memory for things learnt, read, experienced, or heard.'[17]

In an influential essay entitled 'Digital Maoism', veteran internet guru Jaron Lanier explains that collaborative intelligence makes for feeble consensus formation. On his own experience of contributing to Wikis he writes: 'What I've seen is a loss of insight and subtlety, a disregard for the nuances of considered opinions, and an increased tendency to enshrine the official or normative beliefs of an organization.'[18]

16. Andrew Keen, 'The second generation of the Internet has arrived. It's worse than you think', *Weekly Standard*, 15.2.2006, http://www.weeklystandard.com/Content/Public/Articles/000/000/006/714fjczq.asp (accessed 5 June 2007).

17. See also Andrew Keen, *The Cult of the Amateur: How Today's Internet is Killing Our Culture* (New York: Doubleday, 2007).

18. Jaron Lanier, *Edge - Digital Maoism - The Hazards of the New Online Collectivism*. 30.5.2006, http://www.edge.org/3rd_culture/lanier06/lanier06_index.html (accessed 5 June 2007).

Other critics have little faith in the quality of valorisation via collective intelligence. Information professionals still see a major role for themselves in the future. 'It's the role of professional journalists to make a selection from the huge media supply,' writes Geert-Jan Bogaerts (*de Volkskrant*'s internet manager) on his weblog. 'In a newspaper or a radio or television newscast, connections are made that listeners or viewers would not make of their own accord.'[19]

19. Martijn de Waal, Theo van Stegeren, Maarten Reijnders (eds.), *Jaarboek De Nieuwe Reporter 2007. Journalistiek in Nederland: onderweg, maar waarheen?* (Apeldoorn: Uitgeverij Het Spinhuis, 2007), 159.

A second barrage of criticism concerns the commercial character of the institutions that facilitate the media ecology. Critics like Trebor Scholz, Andrew Keen again, and David Nieborg point out that many of the Web 2.0 tools were developed by companies like Google, Amazon and internet start-ups. By setting up lists, voting on articles or commentaries, media consumers undeniably influence the media ecosystem.[20] But, Nieborg wonders rhetorically, 'the big question is, who benefits from large groups of consumers investing their precious time and insight in, say, writing reviews for the Amazon web store?' On *De Nieuwe Reporter*, he argues that there is a fundamental difference

20. Although that influence is not very great as yet. An analysis by Hitwise, a research agency, shows that aggregation services like Google News and Digg play a modest filtering role. Only 5 per cent of all visits to the websites of American broadcast and print media are generated by this kind of service. A much bigger proportion, 12 per cent, is generated by portal sites. In particular, the MSNBC news site (a joint venture by NBC and Microsoft) profited from referrals on the MSN portal site, the default homepage of the Internet Explorer browser. An even bigger proportion, almost a quarter, is generated by standard search engines like Google.

between 'consumers who generate value for companies like *Amazon* with their contributions' and 'users who write a *Wikipedia* entry or maintain their own blog'. [21]

21. David Nieborg, 'Een lange staart is goud waard', *De Nieuwe Reporter*. 31.8.2006. http://www.denieuwereporter.nl/?p=544 (accessed 5 June 2007).

Both Lawrence Lessig and Henry Jenkins have additional worries about copyright. The copyright system turns cultural symbols into the property of commercial institutions and in a media ecology it obstructs the process of encoding. Authority passes to the film studios, publishers or television networks who determine which 'recodings' fans may legally publish.

Yet other critics point out that parallel with the rise of the media ecology is a process of media concentration. The great paradox of contemporary journalism, write the editors of the American *State of the Media* report, is that more and more titles tackle fewer and fewer topics. On an average day in 2005 researchers counted 14,000 references to news items on Google News. On closer analysis it turned out that those many thousands of sources dealt with only 14 different topics. A very small number of media companies and press agencies supply the content circulating around the media ecosystem. Bloggers, the report concluded, may well add new commentaries, but they add few completely new topics. [22] These criticisms are not so much about the developments themselves, which (apart from media concentration) are often viewed as favourable. Rather, they concern the

22. http://www.stateofthenewsmedia.org/2006/narrative_overview_eight.asp?cat=2&media=1 (accessed 21 May 2007).

commercial framework within which those developments take place. Why are no public alternatives being developed in which collective and collaborative filtering systems benefit society instead of the market? And how can we prevent production in the ecosystem also falling into the hands of a small group of big media companies?

A third group of critics warns against cultural fragmentation. Origgi may predict that systems of collaborative intelligence will give rise to new democratic canons, but in the end that system rests on a willingness to engage in debate. But doesn't the internet encourage people to simply introduce their own canon alongside existing ones? As well as Wikipedia, there is now Conservapedia where collaborators are working, for example, on a canon of evolutionary theory from a very different perspective. Henry Jenkins warns of the need for a careful balance between mainstream and niche media. As he sees it, the decline of the mainstream media might even pose a threat to the integrity of the public sphere: 'Expanding the potentials for participation represents the greater opportunity for cultural diversity. Throw away the powers of broadcasting and one has only cultural fragmentation.' [23] Collective filters that determine what we collectively consider important are no match for that.

23. Jenkins, *Convergence Culture*, op. cit. (note 2), 257.

For their part, Blanken and Deuze warn that far-reaching personalization can lead to tunnel vision: 'The successors of Digg and Google will know our preferences, our weaknesses and our passions and will put together a media menu precisely tailored to our taste and expectations. And all sorts of things will be lost as a result. Our horizons will narrow.'[24]

24. Blanken and Deuze, *Pop-up*, op. cit. (note 10).

Once again, this appears to be an ethical rather than a technological issue. For supposing that this kind of intelligent software were to be developed, it would also be able to determine what we *should* regard as important, in the same way that newspaper editors do now, wouldn't it? Clearly, the danger lies not so much with the technology but with ourselves – the danger that, presented with the possibility, we will indulge our narcissism.

In *The Wealth of Networks*, Benkler rejects such criticism. He concedes that there are two camps in the American blogosphere, the conservatives and the liberals. But, he maintains, 15 per cent of the links connect sites 'across the political divide'.[25] To which one could reply that 'linking' is not 'bridging' and counting is not the same as interpreting. A snarky link to an opponent doesn't generate a discussion, for example, but serves rather to vindicate one's own group.

25. Benkler, *The Wealth of Networks*, op.cit. (note 8), 248.

People Power 2.0

Nonetheless, some of Benkler's conclusions have merit. The image of the public sphere on the internet that emerges from his work is not a fixed, locatable place like the opinion page in a newspaper. This public sphere develops wherever the public happens to be and that public can converge at different points in time and in different places – usually at moments when several parties join forces around a particular issue. In a media ecology, thanks to the complex system of links and peer-to-peer groups, a crowd can be mobilized in a short period of time, a phenomenon also known as 'adhocracy'. 'While there is enormous diversity on the internet, there are also mechanisms and practices that generate a common set of themes, concerns and public knowledge around which a public sphere can emerge.'[26]

26. Ibid., 256.

An often-cited case study of an example of an adhocracy may help to clarify the way the ecosystem works and at the same time guard us against an overly technologically deterministic outlook. The study concerns two 'revolutions' that took place on exactly the same spot – the Epifanio de los Santos Avenue (EDSA for short) in Manila – 15 years apart. In 1986, President Marcos fled the Philippines after angry crowds had protested against his regime for four days. In 2001 there was another four-day demonstration on this avenue in the centre of Manila. On this occasion the target was President Estrada, who was forced to resign after the collapse of his impeachment trial for corruption.

In the first People Power movement (as the events were later labelled), the radio and a hierarchical social organization played a major role in mobilizing the crowd. On 22 February 1986, Radio Veritas, a Catholic station not under the direct control of the Marcos regime, broadcast a press conference at which two military leaders declared that Marcos had cheated during the recent presidential elections. That same day, via the popular archbishop Jaime Cardinal Sin, the radio station called on listeners to support the protest against the president and to gather on EDSA. There the demonstrators held radios clamped to their ears. And even after the section of the army that had remained loyal to the president had knocked down its main transmitter, Radio Veritas continued to play a role. Via a standby – albeit weaker – transmitter, the station continued to broadcast reports, including the latest government troop movements.

Descriptions of People Power II in 2001 usually assign a central role to the mobile telephone and to the decentralized peer-to-peer networks that can be formed with it. This, for example, is how Howard Rheingold describes the events of that year in his book *Smart Mobs*: 'Opposition leaders broadcast text messages and within seventy-five minutes of the abrupt halt of the impeachment proceedings 20,000 people showed up. . . . More than 1 million Manila residents [were] mobilized and coordinated by waves of text messages . . . On January 20, 2001 President Joseph Estrada of the Philippines became the first head of state in history to lose power to a smart mob.'[27] According to Rheingold, the protest rapidly escalated into a mass movement because those involved were texting messages like 'Go 2 EDSA, Wear Black 2 mourn d death f democracy. Noise barrage at 11 pm'[28] to everybody in their mobile phone address book. Telephone company Globe

27. Howard Rheingold, *Smart Mobs* (Cambridge, MA: Basic Books, 2002), 158-160.

28. Manuel Castells, Jack Linchuan Qiu, Mireia Fernandéz-Ardèvol and Araba Sey, *Mobile Communication and Society* (Cambridge, MA: MIT Press, 2007), 188.

Telecom sent 45 million text messages that day, almost twice as many as normal.[29] The network became so overloaded that telephone companies erected extra mobile transmitters around EDSA. Other decentralized 'grassroots media' are also credited with a role. Criticism, often in the form of parodies of Estrada, were circulated via email, and the online forum E-lagada claimed to have collected 91,000 signatures against President Estrada's government.[30]

29. Ibid., 189.

30. Ibid., 188.

But is it really true, as Castells, Fernández Ardèvol and Qiu rightly ask, that the uprising succeeded thanks to 'invincible technology' that resulted in 'each user becoming his or her own broadcasting station: a node in a wider network of communication that the state could not possibly monitor much less control'.[31] In other words, was this an adhocracy facilitated by new processes of valorisation whereby the mobilization was the result not of an appeal by an authority via the mass media but of the collective intelligence of a smart mob?

31. Ibid., 191.

Many of those who took part in the demonstration think that it was. In 'The Cell Phone and the Crowd: Messianic Politics in the Contemporary Philippines', Vicente Rafael quoted several reactions from newspapers and online discussions.[32] 'The mobile telephone is our weapon,' said an unemployed construction worker. 'The mobile telephone was like the fuse of the powder keg, with which the uprising was kindled.' Another, in the same

32. Vincente Rafael, 'The Cell Phone and the Crowd: Messianic Politics in the Contemporary Philippines', *Public Culture* V. 15 # 3 (2003).

upbeat prose: 'As long as your battery's not empty, you're "in the groove", and you feel militant.' And: 'The information and calls that reached us by way of text and e-mail was what brought together the organized as well as unorganized protests. From our homes, schools, dormitories, factories, churches, we poured into the streets there to continue the trial [against Estrada].'

Rafael sees such comments in a broader cultural context. In the late 1990s, mobile phones became incredibly popular in the Philippines, especially after Globe introduced prepaid subscriptions with cheap text messaging. Owners talk about their phone as a 'new limb' with a very important property: wherever they are, they can always be somewhere else at the same time. In any given social setting they can communicate with other members of a self-selected group that is not physically present. Conversely, the telephone can be used as a unifying element during mass gatherings: 'While telecommunication allows one to escape the crowd, it also opens up the possibility of finding oneself moving in concert with it, filled with its desire and consumed by its energy.'[33] Sending text messages turns into

33. Ibid.

a symbolic practice surrounded by an imagined community which in the Philippines has been labelled 'Generation TXT'. As such, sending text messages can be seen as a contemporary equivalent of waving a flag in revolutionary colours.

But were Rheingold and others right in claiming that the mobile phone represented a shift in the structure of authority? This is where we must be on our guard against technological determin-ism. As Castells et al. show, there are several objections to the claim that the mobile phone alone was responsible for toppling Estrada. The state's power had already been weakened, thus reducing the government's ability to respond to the uprising. In other countries where the state is much stronger, we see far fewer successful political smart mobs. In China, for instance, the authorities are still able to contain protest demonstrations and their effects. Another factor is the economic embeddedness of the telecom services. A strong state would probably have been able to disable the sms network, in the same way as the Radio Vertias transmitter was knocked out in 1986. In reality, the telecom companies, who saw their sms revenues double that day, set up extra mobile transmitters at EDSA.

So it would be going too far to identify the mobile phone and the cultural practice of text messaging as solely responsible for the revolution. That said, the kind of social networks the cell phone made possible in the cultural, political and economic conditions in the Philippines did play a role. Interesting in this context is Rafael's analysis of a contribution to a discussion forum by the initially sceptical Bart Guingona, who described how he started to believe in the power of sms peer-to-peer networking during the demonstrations. He was part of a group of people who organized one of the first protest gatherings. When someone suggested sending an invitation via sms, he doubted whether it would work without being validated by an authority. A priest who was involved in the preparations suggested enlisting

Radio Veritas in a repeat of 1986. In the end, it was decided to send a test sms. When Guingona turned on his phone the next morning it was to find that friends and friends of friends had forwarded the message en masse, including to his own inbox: indirectly he had got his own sms back in threefold.[34]   34. Ibid.

Guingona, Rafael explained, had little faith in the power of text messages because he saw them as equivalent to rumour. In order to be credible, the message would need to be legitimated by a traditional authority. This proved to be a misconception. An sms is no isolated message from an unknown source of dubious status, but a message from a known sender within one's own social network. And that remains the case, even when the message is forwarded for the second, third or thirtieth time. Validation of the message occurs not via an authority but via an accumulation of individual decisions whether or not to forward the message within the network. Rafael: 'The power of texting here has less to do with the capacity to open interpretation and stir public debate as it does with compelling others to keep the message in circulation. Receiving a message, one responds by repeating it. One forwards it to others who, it is expected, will do the same. Repeatedly forwarding messages, one gets back one's exact message, mechanically augmented but semantically unaltered.'[35]   35. Ibid.

What this case shows is that the peer-to-peer networks played a role in the process of validation and mobilization in Manila's public space around an issue. At the same time this exam-ple shows that if we are to understand such phenomena properly, we mustn't become fixated on the technology, or on processes of collective and collaborative intelligence. Instead we must look at the entire context of an event and at the various related elements of the ecosystem. It was the interaction between different levels of scale of the mass media, the niche media and the p2p networks that in this instance created an adhocracy around the issue of the deadlocked corruption proceedings. But this is not to say that a similar technological constellation would have the same outcome in a different context. Or that this technology automatically leads to processes that are beneficial to democracy. Football hooligans who use their mobile phones to mobilize and coordinate their brawls are also examples of adhocracies and smart mobs.

Which brings us back to the initial question. We can now say that the role of traditional gatekeepers, though declining, is a long way from being played out. The role of filters based on computer algorithms that aggregate and analyse social and cultural practices is increasing. Alongside these forms of collective intelligence, we are also seeing processes of collaborative intelligence. All these developments offer possibilities for creating adhocracies around particular issues. But they can equally well lead to media hypes, and they may still be thwarted by a traditional authority like the state. Commercial concerns often play a role in facilitating such processes and public alternatives do not exist in every area. The technology-based values of companies like Google may even result in media producers adapting their output to those values. And there is a further danger of such adhocracies breaking away from the greater whole and cultivating their own canon.

It is difficult, therefore, to talk about an all-powerful new paradigm. There is no easily localized 'Public Sphere 2.0'. Rather, different and often opposing processes are taking place simultaneously. Yes, new media technologies offer more possibilities for controlling the state and the mass media or for self-organization. But this does not necessarily, and certainly not automatically, lead to a better democracy. Additionally, it is important to analyse every case individually and to look at the whole context of the media ecosystem. Who provides what input for which political and/or commercial reasons? What are the motives of institutional organizations involved in this process? How are those motives translated into technology (from software and filter algorithms to hardware) and what are the limiting or empowering consequences of that technology? Then again, how does the bottom-up process of decoding and recoding work? Which particular practices are of importance here? What role do those practices play in the process of valorisation? Only by continually asking these kinds of questions will we be able to get a better grip on the fluid Public Sphere 2.0.

Geert Lovink

Nihilism and the News

Blogging as a Mental Condition

In a recently published book, *Zero Comments: Blogging and Critical Internet Culture*, Geert Lovink analyses the impact of blogging on the public sphere. This essay is an updated version of one chapter of his book, 'Blogging: The Nihilist Impulse', in which Lovink sees blogging as an attitude aimed at undermining 'the mighty and seductive power of the broadcast media'.[1]

1. Geert Lovink, *Zero Comments: Blogging and Critical Internet Culture* (New York: Routledge, August 2007).

Weblogs or blogs are successors of the '90s internet homepage. They create a mix of the private (online dairy) and the public (PR management of the self). According to *Blog Herald*'s rough estimate, there are 100 million blogs worldwide. In the first half of 2007 *Technorati* was indexing 70 million blogs. It is next to impossible to make general statements about the 'nature' of blogs. Instead of dividing them into proper genres, I will stick to the impossible task of formulating a 'general theory of blogging', starting with the software and menu choices that all bloggers have to deal with. The techno-determinist has to resist the academically correct move to differentiate in categories. Blogs are first and foremost a special effect of the underlying software architecture, no matter whether the chitchat is about cats, chocolate or the war in Iraq.

Instead of looking into the emancipatory potential of blogs, or emphasizing the counter-cultural folklore, I see blogs as part of an unfolding process of 'massification' of the internet after its successive academic and speculative phases. The void after the dotcom crash made way for large-scale, interlinked conversations through freely available automated software with user-friendly interfaces. The blogosphere echoes a collective spirit aimed at creating a public domain, a pre-1992 value that the internet once embodied and that was weakened by the greedy 'virtual class', which was no longer interested in the specificities of the 'media question' and was in the game only to sell out and leave the scene.

Web services like blogs cannot be separated from the output they generate. The politics and aesthetics defined by the first generations of bloggers will characterize the medium for decades to come. Blogs appeared during the late '90s, in the shadow of high-profile online services such as e-commerce and the portal.[2] Blog culture was not developed enough to be dominated by MBA consultants with its hysterical demo-or-die-now-or-never mentality. Blogs first appeared as casual conversations around a link that could not easily be commodified. Building a laid-back parallel world made it possible for blogs to form the crystals (a term coined by Elias Canetti) from which millions of blogs grew and, around 2003, reached critical mass.

Let's have a close look at what happens when we 'blog'. A blog is commonly defined as a frequent, chronological publication of personal thoughts and web links, a mixture of what is happening in a person's life and what is happening on the web and in the world out there.[3] A blog allows for the easy creation of new pages: text and images are entered into an online form (which usually has room for the title, the category and the body of the article), and the form is submitted. As user, you stare at an empty web form and start to record your thoughts. When you're finished – on average, after writing 250 words – you push the submit button. Automated templates add the article to the home page, creating the new full article page (permalink) and putting

2. See Rebecca Blood's history of blogs, written in September 2000: http://www.rebeccablood.net/essays/weblog_history.html.

3. See http://www.marketingterms.com/dictionary/blog/.

Weblogs cumulative: March 2003-March 2007 (source: www.technorati.com)

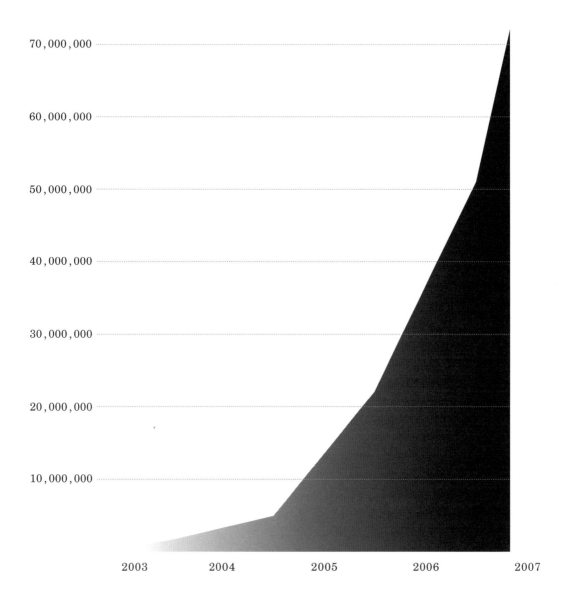

the article into the appropriate date- or category-based archive. Because of the tags that the author includes in each posting, blogs let us filter by date, category, author or a similar attribute. In most cases, the blog administrator is allowed to invite and add other authors, whose permission and access are easily managed.[4]

4. Taken from *Wikipedia*'s blog definition (accessed December 21, 2005).

Blogging in the post-9/11 period closed the gap between internet and society. Whereas dotcom suits dreamt of mobbing customers flooding their sites, blogs were the actual catalysts that led to the worldwide democratization of the Net. To the same degree that 'democratization' means 'engaged citizens', it also implies 'normalization' (as in setting of norms) and 'banalization'. We can't separate these elements and enjoy only the interesting bits. According to Jean Baudrillard, we're living in the 'universe of integral reality'. 'If there was in the past an upward transcendence, there is today a downward one. This is, in a sense, the second Fall of Man Heidegger speaks of: the fall into banality, but this time without any possible redemption.'[5] If you can't cope with high degrees of irrelevance, blogs won't be your cup of tea.

5. Jean Baudrillard, *The Intelligence of Evil or the Lucidity Pact* (Oxford/New York, 2005), 25.

Relationship with the News Industry

There is a presumption that blogs have a symbiotic relationship with the news industry. This thesis is not uncontested. A Pew/Internet survey of blogs clearly showed the diversity of topics bloggers are interested in. The report con-cluded that '37% of bloggers say that the primary topic of their blog is "my life and experiences". Other topics ran distantly behind: 11% of bloggers focus on politics and government; 7% focus on entertainment; 6% focus on sports; 5% focus on general news and current events; 5% focus on business; 4% on technology; 2% on religion, spirituality or faith and additional smaller groups who focus on a specific hobby, a health problem or illness.'[6] These figures clearly indicate that there is no self-evident relation between blogging and journalism.

6. Pew/Internet, Bloggers: A portrait of the Internet's new storytellers, posted on July 19, 2006. URL: http://www.pewinternet.org/PPF/r/186/report_display.asp.

To label blogs as 'citizen journalism' is a noble act but suggests that bloggers see themselves as 'amateurs' or wannabe journalists. I would say that this is not the case. The lost discipline of hypertext, for instance, points at other motives. Hypertext scholars track blogs back to 1980s hypercards and the 1990s online literature wave, in which clicking from one document to the next is the central activity of the reader. If the act of blogging is centred on linking, they could be right. For some reason, however, the hypertext undercurrent lost out, and what remains is an almost self-evident equation between blogs and the news industry.

It is not easy to say whether blogs operate inside or outside the media industry. To position the blog medium inside the news business could be seen as opportunistic, whereas others see this as a clever career move. There is also a 'tactical' aspect. The blogger-equals-journalist might get protection from such a label in case of censorship and repression.

Despite countless attempts to feature blogs as alternatives to the mainstream media, they are often more precisely described as 'feedback channels'. The act of 'gatewatching' (Axel Bruns) the mainstream media outlets does not necessarily result in reasonable comments that will be taken into account. In the category 'insensitive' we have a wide range, from hilarious to mad, sad and sick. What CNN, newspapers and radio stations the world over have failed to do – namely, to integrate open, interactive messages from their constituencies – blogs do for them. To 'blog' a news report doesn't mean that the blogger sits down and thoroughly analyses the discourse and the circumstances, let alone checks the facts. To blog merely means to point quickly to a news item through a link and to write a few sentences that explain why the blogger found this or that factoid interesting, remarkable or debatable.

I would define blog entries as hastily written personal musings, sculptured around a link or event. In most cases bloggers simple do not have the time, the skills and the financial means for proper research. There are collective research blogs at work on specific topics, but these are rare. What ordinary blogs create is a dense cloud of 'impressions' around a topic. Blogs test. They allow you to see whether or not your audience is still awake and receptive. In that sense, we could also say that blogs are the outsourced, privatized test beds, or rather unit tests[7], of the big media.

7. Ed Phillips from San Francisco reports that 'unit testing is now *de rigueur* in the software world and just as it would be hard to imagine a major software effort without unit testing, it is now hard to imagine big media without the blogosphere' (email, 27 March 2006).

New Formats

Nonetheless, boundaries between the media sphere and the blogosphere are fluid. A detailed social analysis would uncover, most likely, a grey area of freelance media-makers moving back and forth. From the outset, journalists working for 'old media' ran blogs. So how do blogs relate to independent investigative journalism? At first glance, they look like oppositional or potentially supplementary practices. Whereas the investigative journalist works months, if not years, to uncover a story, bloggers look more like an army of ants contributing to the great hive called 'public opinion'. Bloggers rarely add new facts to a news story. They find bugs in products and news reports but rarely 'unmask' spin, let alone come up with well-researched reports.

Cecile Landman – a Dutch investigative journalist, supporter of Iraqi bloggers and activist in the Streamtime campaign – knows both worlds. 'Journalists . . . need to make a living too. They can't put just anything on-line. Bloggers don't seem to bother too much about this, and that does create a conflict.' According to Landman, blogging is changing the existing formats of information. People are getting bored with the given formats, which 'don't catch up with the news anymore, it no longer glues on their cervical memory stick. It is like a song that you have listened to too often, or . . . a commercial advertisement: you hear it, you can even sing the words, but they are without meaning. Mainstream media start to grasp this. They have begun to search for new formats in order to attract readers (read: advertisers)'[8] – and blogs are but a small chapter in this transformation.

Blogs are not anonymous news sites, they are deeply personal. Blog software does a wonderful trick: it constitutes subjectivity. The blogger becomes an individual (again). Even if we blog together, we still answer to the Call of the Code to tell something about ourselves as unique persons. Blogs lure us away from writing press releases or impersonal observations. As Dave Winer so precisely defines it, a weblog is 'the voice of a person'. It is a digital extension of oral traditions more than a new form of writing.[9] Through blogging, news is transformed from a lecture into a conversation. Blogs echo rumour and gossip, conversations in cafés and bars, on squares and in corridors. They record 'the events of the day' (Jay Rosen). Today's 'recordability' of situations is such that we are no longer upset when computers 'read' all our moves and expressions (sound, image, text) and 'write' them into strings of zeros and ones. In that sense, blogs fit into the wider trend in which all our movements and activities are monitored and stored. In the case of blogs, this is carried out not by some invisible and abstract authority but by the subjects themselves, who record their everyday lives.[10]

8. Geert Lovink, 'Interview with Cecile Landman', 17 January 2006. URL: http://www.networkcultures.org/weblog/archives/2006/01/support_iraqi_b.html.

9. Nick Gall: 'A lot of the media are thinking about blogs as a new form of publishing but it's really a new form of conversation and a new form of community.' In: David Kline and Dan Burstein, *blog!* (New York: CDS Books, 2005), 150.

10. Source: *Telepolis*, 27 December 2005. Wolf-Dieter Roth, 'Mein blog liest ja sowieso kein Schwein'. URL: http://www.heise.de/tp/r4/artikel/21/21643/1.html.

Shocklogs

The 2004 blog hype – later eclipsed by the MySpace, YouTube and Second Life waves – could not measure up to the late '90s dotcom hysteria. The economic and political landscape was simply too different. What interests me in this case was the often-heard remark that blogs were cynical and nihilist. Instead of brushing off this accusation, I ran both keywords through the systems to test if it they were hardwired values consolidated inside Blog Nation. Instead of portraying bloggers as 'an army of Davids', as Instapundit blogger Glenn Reynolds suggests,[11] it might be better to study the techno-mentality of users and not presume that bloggers are underdogs on a mission to beat Goliath. An additional reason is the ongoing popularity of 'shocklogs' like the Dutch GeenStijl ('no style'), which in 2007 won the prize for the best Dutch weblog for the second time.

11. Glenn Reynolds, *An Army of Davids: How Markets and Technology Empower Ordinary People to Beat Big Media, Big Government, and Other Goliaths* (Nashville: Nelson Current, 2006).

Dutch 'shocklogs' are an interesting subgenre of what professional optimists like Dan Gillmor call 'We Media'. Shocklogs deliberately position themselves on the border of the news industry. This is participatory culture, but with an unwelcome, nasty outcome. Shocklog entries are written to test the boundaries of the politically correct consensus culture of Western media. According to a (deleted) Wikipedia entry, shocklogs are 'weblogs that use shock and slander to sling mud at current affairs, public individuals and institutions. Authors of shocklogs usually comment on an item in a provoking and insulting way, often resulting in even more seriously offensive comments, such as threats of rape and murder. Occasionally shocklogs will incite the reader to undertake some (online) action, usually in the nature to harass or harm a specific target.'[12]

The largest shocklogs in the Netherlands are Geenstijl, Jaggle, Retecool and Volkomenkut. Unique visitors to these sites are estimated to be 25,000 to 38,000 a day. Shocklogs, also called *treiterlogs* in Dutch, do more than post offensive content; they also draw a crowd of people often interested in expressing their frustrations. These are your average outsides who feel excluded by the progressive-liberal establishment. In many cases the delicate topics discussed on such sites reflect current sentiments in Dutch society, in particular attitudes towards Muslims and other minorities. One example is the community's response to messages posted regarding the murder of Dutch film director Theo van Gogh in November 2004. When it became clear that the suspect had a Moroccan background, and that his actions were rooted in his radical Islamic beliefs, discussions on various shocklogs got overheated. The assassination of Theo van Gogh, who had had experience in posting controversial statements on his own blog, led to numerous online debates peppered with explicit and even racist comments.

12. The *Wikipedia* entry is no longer available, but the initial content has been copied and posted on various websites and can also be found on the web archive of the nettime-l list. Early 2007 there were some discussions and postings on nettime about 'shocklogs', see for instance 17 and 22 January, 2, 8 and 9 February, and 10 March 2007.

It would be ridiculous to denounce bloggers collectively as cynics or nihilists. Cynicism, in this context, is not a character trait but a techno-social condition. The argument is not that bloggers are predominantly cynics in nature or conviction, or vulgar exhibitionists who lack restraint. What is important to note is the *Zeitgeist* into which blogging as a mass practice emerged. Net cynicism is a cultural spin-off of blogging software, hardwired in a specific era; it is the result of procedures such as login, link, edit, create, browse, read, submit, tag and reply. Some would judge the mere use of the term 'cynicism' as blog-bashing. So be it. Again, we're not talking about an attitude here, let alone a shared lifestyle. Net cynicism no longer believes in cyberculture as an identity provider with related entrepreneurial hallucinations. It is constituted by cold enlightenment as a post-political condition and by confession as described by Michel Foucault. People are taught that being liberated requires them to 'tell the truth', to confess all to someone (priest, psychoanalyst, weblog), and that this truth-telling will somehow set them free.[13]

Exhibitionism equals empowerment. Saying aloud what you think or feel, in the manner of de Sade, is not only an option – in the liberal sense of 'choice' – but an obligation, an immediate impulse to respond in order to be out there, with everybody else.

13. Taken from the Foucault Dictionary Project: http://users.california.com/~rathbone/foucau10.htm.

There is a quest for truth in blogging. But it is truth with a question mark. Truth has become an amateur project, not an absolute value, sanctioned by higher authorities. A new interpretation of the more common definition of cynicism might call it 'the unpleasant way of performing the truth'.[14] The internet is not a religion or a mission in and of itself. For some, it turns into an addiction, but one that can be healed like any other medical problem. The post-dotcom/post 9-11 condition borders on 'passionate conservatism' but, in the end, rejects dotcom's petit bourgeois morals and its double standards of cheating and hiding, cooking the books and being rewarded with fat pay checks. The question is, therefore: how much truth can a medium bear? Knowledge is sorrow, and 'knowledge society' propagators have not yet taken this into account.

14. http://www. cynical-c.com/.

In the context of the internet, it is not evil – as Rüdiger Safranski suggested – that is the 'drama of freedom', but triviality. This triviality is a direct result of the abundance of resources made available to those with access to a computer and the internet. The freedom of the press in the 18th through the 20th centuries, if it existed in the first place, had to deal with a (relative) scarcity of paper, typesetting equipment, radio frequencies, and access to satellites and other distribution channels. The freedom of shocklogs, as seen from a historical perspective, remains unprecedented. But, as Baudrillard states, 'All of our values are simulated. What is freedom? We have a choice between buying one car or buying another car?'[15] To continue Baudrillard's line of thinking, we could say that blogs are a gift to humankind that no one

15. Interview with Jean Baudrillard by Deborah Solomon, 20 November 2005, *New York Times Magazine*.

needs. This is the true shock. Did anyone order the development of blogs? It is impossible to simply ignore blogs and live the comfortable lifestyle of a 20th-century 'public intellectual'. Like Michel Houellebecq, bloggers are trapped by their own inner contradictions in the Land of No Choice. *The Times of London* noted that Houellebecq 'writes from inside alienation. His bruised male heroes, neglected by their parents, cope by depriving themselves of loving interactions; they project their coldness and loneliness on to the world.'[16] Blogs are perfect projection fields for such an undertaking.

16. Douglas Kennedy, quoted by Maya Jaggi in *The Guardian*, 5 November 2005. URL: http://books. guardian.co.uk/depart- ments/generalfiction/ story/0,,1627808,00.html.

Cosmos of Micro-Opinions

We're operating in a post-deconstructionist world in which blogs offer a never-ending stream of confessions, a cosmos of micro-opinions attempting to interpret events beyond well-known 20th-century categories. The nihilist impulse emerges as a response to the increasing levels of complexity within interconnected topics. There is little to say if all occurrences can be explained through the politically correct lenses of post-colonialism, class analysis, environmentalism and gender perspective. Blogging arises against this kind of 'correct' analysis, through which not a great deal can be said any more. As many have already noticed, blogs revolt against the nihilist manipulations of global news corporations, but that's only half the story.

Blogs express personal fear, insecurity and disillusion – anxieties looking for partners-in-crime. We seldom find passion (except for the act of blogging itself). Often blogs unveil doubt and insecurity about what to feel, what to think, believe and like. Bloggers' confessions carefully compare magazines and review traffic signs, nightclubs and T-shirts. This stylized uncertainty circles around the general assumption that blogs ought to be biographical while simultaneously reporting on the world outside. Their emotional scope is much wider than that of other media, thanks to the informal atmosphere of blogs. Mixing the public with the private is constitutional here. What blogs play with is an emotional register that runs from boredom to hate to passionate engagement to sexual outrage and back again.

Blogs are witnessing and documenting the diminishing power of the mainstream media, but they have consciously not replaced its ideology with an alternative. Users are tired of top-down communication – yet they have nowhere else to go. 'There is no other world' could be read as a response to the anti-globalization slogan 'Another world is possible'. Alternative or not, there are plenty of stories, observations, pictures, remarks and notes that float around, looking a dozen or so viewers. Caught in the daily grind of blogging, one feels that the Network *is* the alternative. It is not correct to judge blogs merely on the basis of content. Media theory has never taken this approach and here, too, should shy away from this type of evaluation. Blogging is a nihilistic venture precisely because the ownership structure of mass media is questioned and attacked – without providing an answer to the looming crisis. Blogging is a bleed-to-death strategy (*actiones in distans*). Implosion is not the right word. Implosion implies a tragedy and a spectacle that fails to describe this situation. Blogging is the opposite of spectacle. It is flat (and yet meaningful). Blogging is not a digital clone of the 'letter to the editor'. Instead of complaining and arguing, the blogger assumes the perversely pleasurable position of media observer.

Commenting on mainstream culture, on its values and products, should be read as an open withdrawal of attention. The eyeballs that once patiently looked at all reports and ads have gone on strike. According to the utopian blog philosophy, mass media are doomed. Their role will be taken over by 'participatory media'. The terminal diagnosis has been made, and it states that closed top-down organizations no longer work, that knowledge cannot be 'managed', and that today's work is collaborative and networked. Despite continual warning signs, however, the system successfully continues to (dys)function. Is top-down really on its way out? Where are the origins of the Hegelian certainty that the old media paradigm will be overthrown? There is little factual evidence of its demise. It is this ongoing state of affairs that causes nihilism, and not revolutions, to occur.

Seen in the light of established structures of meaning, blogs bring on decay. Each new blog is supposed to add to the fall of the media system that once dominated the 20th century. We cannot downplay their supposed influence by saying that blogs are merely a 'secondary' public realm. What blogs, wikis and social-network sites question is the hegemony. Once hegemony is undermined, it cannot be repaired easily, and to a greater and greater degree power will have to rely on force. Mainstream media are losing their self-evidence. This process is not one marked by a sudden explosion. The erosion of mass media cannot be traced easily in figures indicating the stagnant sales and declining readership of newspapers. In many parts of the world television is still on the rise. What's declining is the Belief in the Message – this is the nihilist moment, and blogs facilitate the culture as no platform has ever done before. Sold by the positivists as 'citizen media' commentary, blogs assist users in their crossing from Truth to Nothingness.

Bloggers are nihilists because they are 'good for nothing'. Posting their messages on nirvana, they turn their futility into a productive force. They are the nothingists who celebrate the death of centralized structures of meaning and ignore accusations that they produce only noise. They are disillusionists whose conduct and opinions are regarded as worthless.[17] The printed and broadcast message has lost its aura. News is consumed as a commodity with entertainment value. Instead of lamenting the ideological colour of the news, as previous generations have done, we blog as a sign of the regained power of the spirit. As a micro-heroic, Nietzschean act of the pyjama

people, blogging grows out of a nihilism of strength, not out of the weakness of pessimism. Instead of presenting blog entries as self promotion, time and again, we should interpret them as decadent artefacts that remotely dismantle the mighty and seductive power of the broadcast media.

17. Justin Cremers, *The Romanticism of Contemporary Theory* (Ashgate: Hants, 2003), 77.

Richard Grusin

Publicity,
Pornography,
or Everyday
Media Practice?

On the Abu Ghraib
Photographs

According to
Richard Grusin,
the reason that
the photographs
from Abu Ghraib
triggered such a
commotion is not
that they cross the
ethical boundaries
of media practice.
He believes that
their similarity
to everyday media
practices of
producing and
circulating digital
images is the cause.

What makes a geopolitical issue a matter of public concern to US and global media? In this essay I address this question by reference to Abu Ghraib, which has almost certainly been the single issue of greatest public media concern that has arisen in the more than four years since the US invaded Iraq in March 2003. Why have the photographs from Abu Ghraib had a public and political impact far greater than, say, the unlawful establishment of a detention centre at Guantanamo Bay, or the policy and practice of 'extraordinary rendition', or the countless other US violations of the Geneva Convention and the bounds of accepted behaviour more generally? From one perspective the answer would appear to be self-evident. Indeed it is precisely self-evidence that underwrites the immediately disturbing nature of the photographs: they themselves are 'self-evident', that is, they provide visual evidence of degrading, brutal torture and violence. The photographs don't lie. Verbal reports of torture at Abu Ghraib and elsewhere had been circulating for some time in early 2004, and the US Army had been investigating criminal abuse at the prison since May 2003. Nonetheless, it was only after an American television 'news-magazine', *60 Minutes II*, showed the now-iconic photos of 'hooded man' and 'leashed man' on prime-time US TV on 28 April 2004, that the mainstream news media, the global public, and the American government were forced to do something about it. The common explanation for the publicity garnered by these photographs has to do with the fact that the events depicted were horrible and that seeing is believing, that visual imagery has a much more powerful impact than verbal accounts do. True enough. Photographs, unlike printed texts, are by their nature public, visible, out in the open. Once they have been released, what they depict can't be ignored.

But might there be another explanation, one that concerns not only the nature of the criminal abuse revealed by the photographs, but also our experience of the photographs as sociotechnical, material artefacts – the way in which their production and circulation were part and parcel of our everyday media practices? Could the powerful and immediate public outcry caused by the release of the photographs be explained not only because the photographs made visible horrible acts of torture, completely out of the ordinary and beyond the pale of acceptable, civilized, humane behaviour, but also because the practice of producing and circulating the Abu Ghraib photographs was continuous with our own acceptable, civilized, everyday, humane media practices? Rather than consider the Abu Ghraib photographs as transparent windows through which we could view unthinkable, horrible practices of torture and humiliation (practices virtually identical to those going on in Guantanamo Bay or elsewhere in occupied Iraq or Afghanistan or at clandestine torture sites around the globe), what would it mean to consider them as sociotechnical artefacts, operating within a premediated network of media practices similar, if not identical, to those practices widespread among students, tourists, parents, petowners, photo-bloggers, and in the military itself? Could it be that what made Abu Ghraib into an issue of worldwide

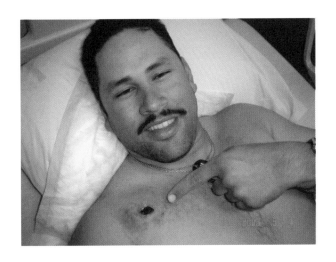

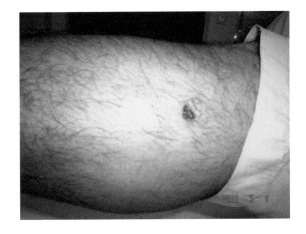

public media attention was not what the photographs revealed about acts of torture and humiliation that were almost universally and immediately understood to be beyond the pale even of military interrogation, but what they revealed about our own media practices, how they operated within our everyday media? Did Abu Ghraib become a matter of world-wide public media concern because the criminal acts of torture performed there by US soldiers were documented and circulated through practices of taking digital photographs, uploading photos on web-sites, and e-mailing those photographs to friends and family that are of a piece with our own everyday practices of photographing our pets, our vacations, or our loved ones, and then sharing these images with friends, family, or strangers via the same media of file-sharing, email, social networking, mobile phones, and the web – practices with which global citizens are becoming increasingly familiar and comfortable?

One approach to answering these questions can be found in the response by Democrat Richard 'Dick' Durbin, then Assistant Minority Leader of the US Senate, after being shown the entire set of photographs from Abu Ghraib in a classified session. Durbin recalls: 'You can't imagine what it's like to go to a closed room where you have a classified briefing, and stand shoulder to shoulder with your colleagues in the Senate, and see hundreds and hundreds of slides like those of Abu Ghraib, most of which have never been publicly disclosed. I had a sick feeling when I left. . . . It was then that I began to have suspicions that something significant was happening at the highest levels of the government when it came to torture policy.'[1] Although objecting to the US military's apparently government-sanctioned practice of torture and humiliation as depicted in the photographs, Durbin is also reacting to the mediality of the photographs themselves, the act of viewing photographic slides standing shoulder to shoulder with his colleagues in the Senate. Interestingly, Durbin does not say 'you can't imagine what it's like to see such horrible acts of torture', but rather 'you can't imagine what it's like to . . . stand shoulder to shoulder with your Senate colleagues and see hundreds and hundreds of these photos'. What he comments on is the humiliation, the embarrassment, of being side-by-side with his Senate colleagues and looking at such photographs, where he might in some other circumstances have stood with many of those same colleagues to look at pictures of their children's weddings or their most recent vacation or a new house they might have bought. Durbin's formulation of his response is not, I would argue, meaningless, but rather points our attention to the connection between the global media publicity garnered by these photographs from Abu Ghraib and their continuity with our everyday media practices.

1. Jane Mayer, 'A Deadly Interrogation', *The New Yorker*, 14 November 2005.

Sexual Component

Shortly after the release of the Abu Ghraib photos, Susan Sontag addressed their status as media artefacts in her powerful essay 'Regarding the Torture of Others', arguing that the horror of the acts of torture depicted in the photographs could not be separated from the horror of the acts of photography themselves.[2] Sontag likens these photographs to those that German soldiers took of the horrors of Nazi concentration camps in the Second World War, or to those taken of lynching victims by Ku Klux Klansman in the USA, who then distributed them to their friends and family as postcards. Furthermore, she recognizes the heightened impact of the widespread possession of digital cameras and the ease of circulating photos across networked media: 'Where once photographing war was the province of photojournalists, now the soldiers themselves are all photographers – recording their war, their fun, their observations of what they find picturesque, their atrocities – and swapping images among themselves and e-mailing them around the globe.' For Sontag, however, what soldiers find 'fun' seems increasingly beyond the pale of what she considers to be moral behaviour, particularly insofar as it seems connected with the prevalence of internet pornography: 'An erotic life is, for more and more people, that whither can be captured in digital photographs and on video. And perhaps the torture is more attractive, as something to record, when it has a sexual component. It is surely revealing, as more Abu Ghraib photographs enter public view, that torture photographs are interleaved with pornographic images of American soldiers having sex with one another. In fact, most of the torture photographs have a sexual theme, as in those showing the coercing of prison-

2. Susan Sontag, 'Regarding the Torture of Others,' *New York Times Magazine*, 23 May 2004.

ers to perform, or simulate, sexual acts among themselves. . . . [M]ost of the pictures seem part of a larger confluence of torture and pornography: a young woman leading a naked man around on a leash is classic dominatrix imagery. And you wonder how much of the sexual tortures inflicted on the inmates of Abu Ghraib was inspired by the vast repertory of pornographic imagery available on the Internet – and which ordinary people, by sending out Webcasts of themselves, try to emulate.'[3]

3. The connection between the Abu Ghraib photographs and pornography has been widespread. See, for example, David Simpson, *9/11: The Culture of Commemoration* (Chicago: University of Chicago Press, 2006); Susan Willis, *Portents of the Real: A Primer for Post-9/11 America* (London/New York: Verso, 2005).

Sontag calls attention to the mediality of the photographs primarily to condemn them for what they reveal about the media environment from which they emerge – or more specifically to condemn the culture that produces both that media environment and the soldiers who inhabit it: 'For the meaning of these pictures is not just that these acts were performed, but that their perpetrators apparently had no sense that there was anything wrong in what the pictures show.' On the one hand she argues that the horror of these images derives in large part from how they function *as photographs*; on the other hand she condemns the Bush administration for thinking that 'the fault or horror lay in the images, not in what they depict'. For Sontag, what these images depict is the corruption of American culture: 'What is illustrated by these photographs is as much the culture of shamelessness as the reigning admiration for unapologetic brutality.' Ironically, the terms of Sontag's condemnation of the Abu Ghraib

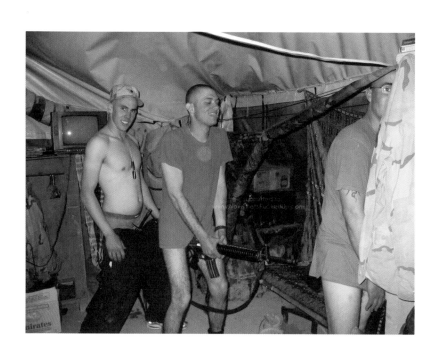

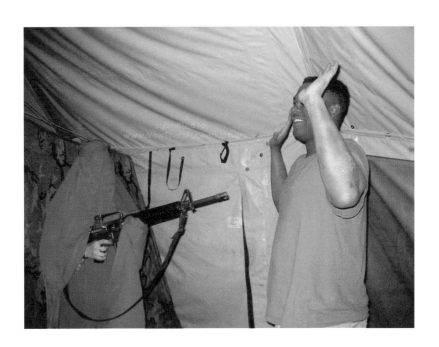

photographs are not very different (at least medialogically) from the morally conservative position that the existence of the Abu Ghraib photographs (if not the torture itself) derives from America's media culture: 'It is hard to measure the increasing acceptance of brutality in American life, but its evidence is everywhere, starting with the video games of killing that are a principal entertainment of boys – can the video game 'Interrogating the Terrorists' really be far behind? – and on to the violence that has become endemic in the group rites of youth on an exuberant kick.[4] In the weeks following the release of the Abu Ghraib photos, such condemnation of US media culture was a staple of conservative Christian media, exemplified in print, televisual, and networked news media by figures like born-again Watergate conspirator Charles Colson or Ted Olsen, former US Solicitor General who successfully represented George W. Bush in Bush v. Gore, the US Supreme Court case that effectively handed Bush the presidency. While on most issues their politics are diametrically opposed, both Sontag and the Christian right acknowledge the importance of thinking about the Abu Ghraib photographs in relation to US media practices. In doing so, however, their arguments focus on content and morality, seeking chiefly to pin the blame on somebody else's media practices, by seeing both the Abu Ghraib torture and the Hollywood media-industrial entertainment complex as beyond the pale of humane, civilized, moral behaviour. My argument about the mediality of the photographs, on the other hand, focuses on the continuity between the formal, technical media practices entailed in the Abu Ghraib photos and our own everyday practices of digital photography. While we cannot ignore the force of the content of the photos in producing public outrage, I want to explain this nearly instantaneous and universal publicity in terms of the medialogical affinities between looking at the Abu Ghraib photos on TV, in the newspaper, or on the web and our everyday practices of seeing photos of friends, family, or co-workers, or looking at photographs in the news, or the affinities between our ordinary digital photographic practices, including posting them on the internet and emailing them to friends, and the media practices engaged in by the soldiers at Abu Ghraib.

4. Simpson and Willis (op. cit. note 3), too, draw the connection between Abu Ghraib and video games.

US Popular Media Culture

Like Sontag, Slavoj Žižek also finds the crux of the matter of the Abu Ghraib photos to lie in their continuity with US popular media culture, characterizing them as depicting 'the obscene underside of US popular culture'.[5] But Žižek's response differs from Sontag's in one crucial respect. Although Sontag might agree that the photographs represent the obscene underside of American culture, she would stop short of Žižek's provocative claim that 'the Iraqi prisoners were effectively being initiated into American culture; they were getting a taste of the obscenity that counterpoints the public values of personal dignity, democracy and freedom'. Even while seeing the events of

5. Slavoj Žižek, 'Between Two Deaths,' *London Review of Books*, 8 July 2004.

Abu Ghraib as initiating the Iraqi prisoners into American culture, however, Žižek would erase the medialogical significance of the photographs. Žižek is unable to see that what makes the Abu Ghraib incident most congruent with everyday American popular culture is its participation in the practices of taking digital photographs and circulating them across premediated sociotechnical networks like the internet or email, and the continuity between these practices and the creation of a media public. While he is right to see the events of Abu Ghraib as continuous with US popular culture, he does not make the connections with media practices explicit, but continues to see the photographs simply as *evidence*. 'The photographs don't lie.' In Žižek's account Abu Ghraib is still understood through a media logic in which photographs or other audiovisual or textual media function as representations of prior events, as records, as evidence, as testimony. What this perspective, and these reports, fail to see is the way in which the photographs do not simply report or testify to immoral or pornographic political, criminal, or military events at Abu Ghraib, but are themselves specific, distinct media events that act with their own political and social consequences.

Žižek's erasure of the mediality of the photographs is most tellingly evident in his discussion of a widely cited quotation from Donald Rumsfeld, in which Rumsfeld distinguishes between 'known knowns', 'known unknowns' and 'unknown unknowns'. Žižek astutely points out that Rumsfeld omits the most important permutation of this sequence, the 'unknown knowns', the 'things we

don't know that we know, which is precisely the Freudian unconscious, the "knowledge which doesn't know itself," as Lacan used to say. . . . The Abu Ghraib scandal shows where the real dangers are: in the "unknown knowns," the disavowed beliefs, suppositions, and obscene practices we pretend not to know about, although they form the flipside of public morality.' Characteristically defining 'unknown knowns' as the Freudian unconscious, Žižek fails to recognize the other kinds of 'knowledge which doesn't know itself' at work in this incident, such as the kinds of knowledge built in to our media practices, into the hardware and software of our digital formats. That is, in addition to those 'unknown knowns' that reside in our unconscious there are any number of other unknown knowns built in to our media practices in ways that we are not aware of, in ways that we do not know that we know – not because they have been repressed or sublimated, but because they are concealed or invisible or unrecognized in everyday practices that we participate in and take for granted. Katherine Hayles makes a similar point in a different context, invoking Nigel Thrift's idea of the *technological unconscious* which refers to 'the everyday habits initiated, regulated, and disciplined by multiple strata of technological devices and inventions, ranging from an artifact as ordinary as a wristwatch to the extensive and pervasive effects of the World Wide Web'.[6] Part of the force of the Abu Ghraib photographs comes precisely from their participation in our technological unconscious – the

6. 'Human cognition', Hayles explains, 'increasingly takes place within environments where human behavior is entrained by intelligent machines through such everyday activities as cursor move-

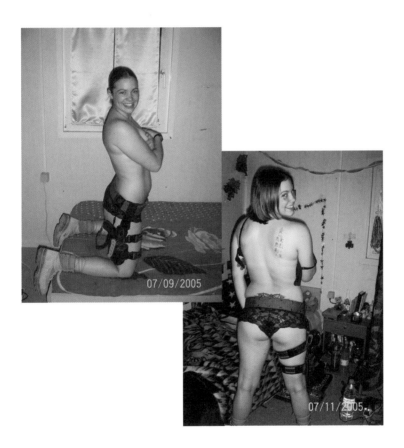

way in which they are integrated within our everyday nonconscious use of technology. What enabled the photographs from Abu Ghraib to create an almost instant issue of global media publicity was not just that they brought to the consciousness of the global public the criminal behaviour of the soldiers involved, but that the consciousness of this behaviour was mediated by the unconscious or nonconscious documentation and circulation of this behaviour across networked media. That is to say, not only does this nonconscious behaviour make the photos into objects of media publicity, but the way in which this behaviour duplicates and intersects with our own premediated media practices adds to their publicity.

NTFU.com

I conclude by turning to a more recent, but much less publicized, controversy over scandalous digital photographs circulated on the Web by US soldiers in Iraq, as a way to dispute the claim that the Abu Ghraib photographs were pornographic and that this was what made them into such objects of media publicity. On 28 September 2005, the *New York Times* reported that the US Army was investigating photographs of Iraqi war

ment and scrolling, interacting with computerized voice tress, talking and text messaging on cell phones, and searching the web to find whatever information is needed at the moment. . . . Enmeshed within this flow of data, human behavior is increasingly integrated with the technological nonconscious through somatic responses, haptic feedback, gestural interactions, and a wide variety of other cognitive activities that are habitual and repetitive and that therefore fall below the threshold of conscious awareness.' N. Katherine Hayles, 'Traumas of Code,' *Critical Inquiry*, Volume 33 (2006), 140; Nigel Thrift, 'Remembering the Technological Unconscious by Foregrounding Knowledges of Position,' *Environment and Planning D: Society and Space* 22 (2004).

dead that had been posted on a website called NowThatsFuckedUp.com (NTFU), owned by an American named Chris Wilson, but hosted in Amsterdam. The *Times* piece refers to a September 20 article in the online *Journalism Review*, the first mainstream US venue to report the story (though it had been investigated by a journalist/blogger associated with the *Christian Science Monitor*, who had learned about it from an Italian blogger and the Italian news agency ANSA). If the story's complex provenance is typical of the interwoven linkages among the blogosphere and networked news media, both print and online, the details of the story itself are less typical, even though it entails many of the same elements raised by the Abu Ghraib photos – graphic photographic images, the violation of Geneva Conventions, the relationship between pornography and violence, the omnipresence of digital cameras. NTFU.com was created as a bulletin board site for (mainly) men to exchange pornographic images of their girlfriends or wives. The site had a structure familiar to anyone who has used similar forums, offering general access boards for the public as well as special access boards for those who provided a certain level of content to the site or who were willing to pay for it. NTFU quickly became popular with soldiers in Iraq and elsewhere, who began to post soft-core pictures of partially dressed, partially nude female soldiers. After the Pentagon blocked access to the site from computers in the field and soldiers in Iraq reported difficulty using their credit cards to access some of the paid features of the site, Wilson decided to offer soldiers free access to these features in exchange for photos from the field. His (ungrammatical and geopolitically uninformed) offer on the site reads: 'As a Thank-You for the work you do and the sacrifices you make I would like to offer you guys who want it the ability to get free access as a SUPPORTER member. [PAR] Just post a picture of you guys hanging out, or saying hi, or of other cool stuff you see while your there. Something like the kinda pictures you would be sending home to your family and friends. Lets see some tanks, guns, the place your living in, some dead Taliban, just anything. I would like to get a glimpse of what you guys are seeing over there and I think everyone here would also. [PAR] In return for your submission I will give you SUPPORTER access in the forums. When I get a few pictures I will setup a special forum called something like 'Pictures From The Field' or something like that and post them all there for people to see.' Many of the soldiers began to post photos that depicted mutilated dead bodies and parts of bodies of Iraqi civilians and insurgents, the kinds of images that the Bush administration as well as the mainstream media sought systematically to prevent the American and global public from seeing.

News stories covering the NTFU incident emphasized its connection with Abu Ghraib and brought up many of the same issues raised by those photographs; nonetheless there was very little public awareness of these photos among the US or global media. Perhaps because it never became a significant media issue, the US Army decided not to pursue disciplinary charges against soldiers who had posted on the site. But on 7 October 2005,

Wilson was arrested in his home in Lakeland, Florida, by Polk county sheriff's deputies on charges of obscenity – not for the photos of Iraqi dead but for the sexually explicit photos on the site. Four days later he was released on bail. On 16 December 2005, his bail was revoked and he was returned to jail because he had continued to operate the website while out on bail. On 13 January of the following year, Wilson pleaded guilty to five misdemeanour obscenity charges in exchange for the state of Florida agreeing to drop its felony charge against him as well as the remaining 295 obscenity counts. He also agreed not to work on any adult websites for the next five years and to shut down his site within 90 days, after which he turned over the URL to the Polk County Sheriff's Office, which now hosts the site with its own anti-pornography message. Wilson has not completely disappeared, however. On 31 March 2006 he opened a short-lived site called barbecuestopper.com, which followed the same bulletin board format as NTFU. He is now the purveyor of the Liberal Blogger, a site that, from the statistical evidence provided, has failed to find its audience. Unlike Abu Ghraib, this incident has dropped out of the media's sight.

I introduce this incident of war photos traded for pornography not to make the now familiar claim that such photos are themselves pornographic. Rather I introduce this incident as a way to think about what makes an issue into a matter of public concern, how media and publicity interact with what I would call our media everyday. Even less than the Abu Ghraib photos, I would argue, these photos of Iraqi dead bear little formal relationship to the photographic conventions of pornography, nor are they designed to arouse their viewers erotically, unlike the photos of female American soldiers and other amateur pornography that was posted on the NTFU site. Following the lead of now-familiar arguments by feminists and critics concerning pornography, Andrea Dworkin and Catharine MacKinnon, Sontag and others equate the photos of Abu Ghraib with pornography based upon the degrading and damaging effect of such images on those who produce the images, those whom the images reproduce, and those who consume them. Although such arguments about the injuriousness of pornography continue to be contested on a variety of fronts, there is a good deal of force to them. And it is hard to imagine anyone who would argue against the damage produced and documented by the Abu Ghraib photos. Nonetheless, if we think about how the Abu Ghraib photos functioned medialogically, about the kinds of work they perform, it is hard to think of them as pornography. Felix Guattari has suggested that in considering behaviour like obsessive hand-washing, we think not of its significance, but of its sensation, 'the feeling that one is in the washing of one's hands'.[7] If we think of the Abu Ghraib photos in this way, I am inclined to agree with Žižek's characterization of them as operating something like trophy photos of fraternity pranks do, as productive not of the feeling that one is being sexually aroused, but of the feeling that one is displaying a trophy. Indeed, irrespective of the sexual components of the behaviour produced

7. Felix Guattari, 'On Machines,' *Journal of Philosophy and the Visual Arts* 6 (1995).

for and documented in the Abu Ghraib photos, I would argue that this was not what made them into global media issues. On the contrary, in the case of NTFU, the conjunction of graphic images of dead bodies and internet pornography helped prevent this issue from becoming a matter of widespread media concern. For while internet pornography is widespread enough that it has become a regular staple of comedy in popular media, the images themselves are not yet visible on US televisual or other popular media. Not unlike dead and mutilated bodies, the naked bodies or those engaged in sexual activity are still kept out of the media public. We know that they are there, we can refer to them humorously or seriously or with shock and outrage, but we are not allowed to see them.

Why did the photographs from Abu Ghraib become an issue of global media publicity? Put most epigrammatically, the media publicity created by the photos from Abu Ghraib lies less in the significance of what they show us than in the sensation they produce, the feeling that in looking at the Abu Ghraib photos we are participating in our ordinary practices of mediality.

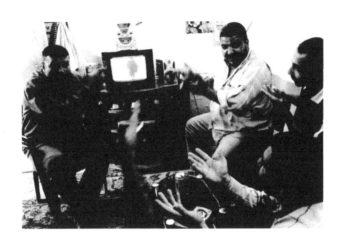

Albert Benschop

Another Life in Cyberspace

The Peculiarities of Second Life

The rise of virtual worlds and the 3D web is accompanied by great transformations in the way in which we communicate and interact, publish and learn, meet people and have fun, do business and are involved in politics. The best-known and most flexible virtual world is Second Life (SL). Web sociologist Albert Benschop explores this digital world and compares the structure of the 3D web with the structure of the old, flat web.

Second Life? I hardly have time to live my first life . . .

The residents of SL interact in a 3D environment. At first sight SL looks like an online role-playing game for a great number of players who are jointly building a virtual existence. Participants create their own digital images. They determine the appearance and character with which they want to live in SL, where you can be whoever you want to be and do whatever you want to do.

The difference between SL and games such as *The Sims Online* and *World of Warcraft* is that the use of SL is not determined by locations and rules that are incorporated in its software. Therefore SL is not a game with pre-programmed story lines: it has no clear-cut playground, no rules of play, no assignments or specific goals. You cannot 'win' in SL.

The environment offered by the inventors is completely *empty*: there are neither subjects nor objects. When SL opened its virtual gates on 23 June 2003 there was nothing; there was no place to go to and nobody to be seen.[1] This empty world is brought to life only when the residents themselves choose a digital alter ego (an avatar) and determine what they want to do in this new world. The residents of SL receive the means to adapt the virtual world to their own wishes and ideas, and subsequently they can share this world with equals. So SL is in the most literal sense of the word a co-creation.

1. A comparison to the biblical story of the creation is there for the taking. 'Now the earth was formless and empty. Darkness was on the surface of the deep.' (*World English Bible*, Genesis 1, verse 2). But this time it is no ethereal god operating as the great creator, but people of flesh and blood creating their own world from behind their keyboards.

SL has a self-developing structure and not a prefabricated one. There is no mission; there are no assignments to be carried out and no bonus points to be gained. Nobody tells you what to do. SL is not a chatroom, not a marketplace, not a site for social networks. It is all in one. SL is a *simulation of reality* within a 3D audiovisual user environment. SL is an electronic living environment or a metaverse (metaphysical universe).

Fantasy World

SL is not a second-hand world but an opportunity to lead a second, virtual life beside (not after!) our local life. At last our longing for rebirth can be realized in a non-infantile way. And this time not as the *idée fixe* of survival beyond the grave, and not with the religious belief in the immortality of the soul (offering only false hope of an eternal hereafter). The second world is not so lofty and can be found in the virtual regions of the here and now. The virtual kingdom belongs to this earth and to people currently alive.

In our first world we act bearing in mind the *materiality* of our body. This body is bound by place and time. In this world we can be in only one place at once (the physical body is indivisible), and we need time to bridge the distance to another place. In the digital world things are completely different. In the digital world we need not surmount natural barriers. Our body remains 'at home', behind the computer screen. In virtual space we are liberated from our corporality and only our avatar manoeuvres, as a more or less fantasized or idealized representation of who we are or who we would like to be.

Empty areas and views from Second Life windows. Visual contribution by Arjan van Amsterdam and Sander Veenhof, DogTime students at the Rietveld Academy in Amsterdam.

Another Life in Cyberspace

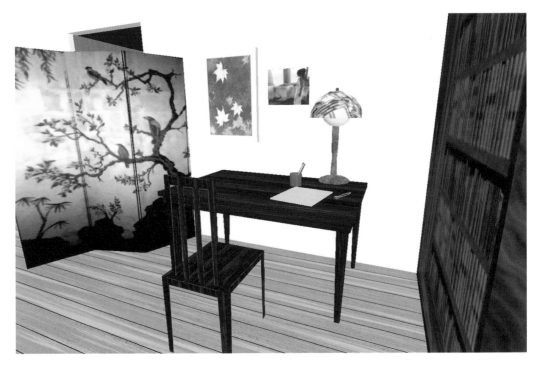

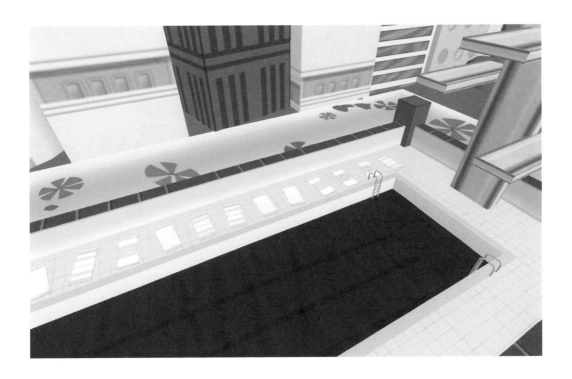

Another Life in Cyberspace

Those who enter a virtual world have the possibility to redefine their *appearance and personality*. This digital representation leaves ample room for the most divergent and extreme fantasies and phobias. It is a large-scale, carnivalesque masquerade in which (almost) nobody is who he or she 'really' is. In SL everybody is really who they pretend to be. Only the digital character and his or her virtual achievements are real.

In SL you can make (nearly) everything imaginable. It is the ultimate fantasy world in which an environment is created in a complete class of its own, with powerful and very flexible instruments. It is a *challenge to be creative*. Those who are not creative get little attention. And that is what the virtual world is mainly about: *attention*, as expressed by the number of visitors and the duration and frequency of their visits.

SL is a completely 3D space, able to imitate the physical world to a very large extent. But it can also differ greatly from the 'real world', if the *imaginative powers* of the designers allow it to do so. The virtual world poses only one limitation: the restriction of human fantasy. The virtual world is in essence a domain where we can indulge our fantasies.

However, in many ways SL is embedded in the daily life of the first world, not only in a psychological and sociocultural respect but also, and especially, in an economic respect. In the fast-growing virtual economy of SL, products, services and land are purchased with 'Linden dollars'. There is a stock exchange where you can buy and sell Linden dollars. In many respects the virtual exchange rate behaves like that of any other foreign currency. More and more companies offer *real life* products and services for sale for Linden dollars. Companies and institutions make use of the advantages SL offers and build their intranets and extranets there. They buy a piece of land in SL and build a virtual office on it. The organization's personnel use this office as a workplace, and it also functions as a marketing and sales outlet for customers.

Digital Spitting Image – Divine Incarnation

Avatars are not of this world.

In the virtual world only the digital alter egos of the residents act. Avatars are of crucial importance to the use of artificial identities in cyberspace. Internet knows many temptations. But the major temptation of SL is its capacity to fulfil a classic and previously unattainable wish: *the desire to start life anew*.[2] SL offers the opportunity to construct a completely new identity. 'In your Second Life, you can look like nearly anyone or anything you want!'

2. In the past the childish desire to be reborn – at any price – was usually transformed into the religious longing for the hereafter. SL offers the chance to fulfil this typically human longing, resulting from the fear of death, in a non-irrational way in the virtual second world.

Some people consider their SL experience a mere fantasy; others regard it as an extension of their off-line personality, which can lead, more than ever, to the blurring of boundaries between reality and fantasy.

One example of blurred boundaries can be found in the construction of avatars. Many SL residents spend a great deal of time on their avatars. Avatars are not simple images but *fantasized images* in which real and imagined aspects of identity merge. In an avatar you articulate how you prefer to present yourself and/or how you prefer to be seen by others.

The construction of an avatar is a divine act of creation. The designer is a god who, in his immense wisdom, creates a new human being that contains a little bit of himself ('after one's own image') and a little imagination. Fantasized, idealized, dreamed, wished for, hoped for, transposed, construed, perverted, cultivated, mirrored, crossbred. 'Avatar' is an accurate characterization of the digital image – in Sanskrit, 'avatar' means 'divine incarnation'.

As true gods we mould our identity to our own will. We model our sex and age, our bodily shape and features, our outerwear and undergarments, our hairstyle and make-up, our adornments (jewels, tattoos) and attributes, our posture and physical movements, our facial expressions and gestures. We can pose as humans but also as animals, dragons, monsters, little robots, cuddly toys or objects.[3] If so desired, we can make ourselves invisible, a condition that allows us to sit somewhere unnoticed and listen in. We can communicate with other avatars by means of text, voice, posture and facial expression.

3. Most residents of SL enjoy indulging their fantasies and 'reinventing' themselves. The more SL grows, the greater the need for realistic avatars. Until now it has been rather complicated to design a photorealistic avatar; at present, however, a few minutes on *Avatar Island* is all that's required to design an alter ego that resembles a photograph.

Peculiarities of the 3D Web

What makes the 3D web so special and so new? How does this new web differ from the by-now-so-familiar flat web? To trace the structural and dynamic peculiarities of 3D virtual spaces, we start with a schematic summary of the differences between the flat and the 3D web (see pp. 74-75). The *structure* of the old web is characterized by independently operating sites in an unlimited virtual space. Sites are mutually connected, in the abstract manner of random dots on a flat surface. In the 3D web, however, separate sites are interdependently linked together in a delineated virtual space. Sites are mutually and concretely connected because they occupy specific places in a 3D space. This structural difference has immediate consequences for the manner of *navigation*. In the 2D web we navigate within and between sites by means of a hyper-transition. Clicking on the magic hyperlink allows us to move with lightning speed from site to site. In the 3D web we can make our avatars travel just as fast over great distances. But the characteristic transfer takes place much more smoothly: we navigate from site to site by having our avatar walk or fly. We no longer operate in an abstract universe in which we move to other sites via hyperlinks, but in a visually marked-out space in which we can make our avatar move.

The difference in structure also has consequences for the way in which we orientate ourselves in the virtual world. In the 2D web, *orientation* occurs primarily with the use of search engines that offer results corresponding with our search terms. In addition, we make use of directories and portals specialized in certain subjects. In the 3D web we orientate ourselves with the help of a human potential for which there is no need in

2D-web

Independently side by side in unlimited virtual space: abstract connection via dots on a flat surface.

STRUCTURE

Invisible to other users: no sense of social presence of others.

Hyper transition: connection by click on magic hyperlink.

NAVIGATION

Not accountable, except in communicative web locations, such as chatrooms, web forums and instant messaging.

Orientation by search engines and directories.

ORIENTATION

Screen name + 2D profiles.

Hypertextuality: textual (re)presentation of information.

INFORMATION

Infinite expansion: no limit of number of local servers and consequently of servers.

Primarily textual communication: no nonverbal communication of emotions except by means of emoticons.

COMMUNICATION

Principally and practically decentred: peer-to-peer model.

Inanimate objects.

ANIMATION

Idiosyncratic power of separate sites: number of incoming links.

3D-web

Dependently together in a delimited virtual space: concrete connection via specific places in 3D space.

——— PRESENCE ———
Visible to other users: sense of social presence – space of proximity.

Smooth transition: connection by movement of avatar, which walks, flies and uses hyper transport.

ACCOUNTABILITY ———
Direct personal accountability: opportunities for self-regulation.

Orientation by spatial imagination.

——— IDENTITY ———
3D avatars.

Hypervisuality: (re)presentation of information; eyes turn into powerful lenses that can focus.[4]

——— EXPANSION ———
Limited expansion: depending on the number of central servers.

Communication in natural language: possibility of nonverbal communication by means of posture, facial expression and gestures.

CENTRALISATION ———
Practically centred: server-client model

Ability to animate all objects.

——— POWER FORMATION ———
Concentrated power of sites on sim: power of sim administrators and property developers.

4. For a few hundred Linden dollars you can buy a camera on SL, allowing you to take pictures or make films in the virtual world. The lenses enable you to zoom in or out.

the flat web: our *spatial imagination*.[5] It allows us to orientate and position ourselves in a spatial living environment, even when this is a merely virtual one. In spite of a flat screen projecting images of a virtual world, we are able to visualize something in three dimensions.[6]

There are other differences that strike the eye. In the 2D web *information* is (re)presented primarily in a textual way, whereas in the 3D web information is (re)presented in a much more visual way or as images. More precisely, in the 3D web hypertextuality and hypervisuality are combined.

This enrichment of the modes of information transfer has immediate consequences for the nature of *communication*. Most communication in the flat web is textual. Although the use of emoticons offers compensation, it remains difficult to convey emotions directly in a nonverbal manner.[7] In the 3D web we can communicate with one another in natural (spoken) language as well. Moreover, our avatars give us the opportunity to communicate nonverbally, by means of posture, facial expression and gestures. Since SL enables us to express feelings and emotions directly, it's possible for activities to assume a greater degree of complexity and ambiguity.[8]

From a socio-scientific perspective, the main difference between the old and the new web lies in the way in which we experience one another's *presence* in virtual space. In the flat web users are invisible to other users. As a rule, visitors to websites do not see which other visitors are simultaneously present on the site. In communicative internet locations – such as chat, IM and web forums – the presence of others is visible only in the form of screen names, written profiles and lifeless, non-animated avatars. In the 3D web, thanks to avatars everyone is instantly visible to all other avatars present in the same delineated space. This perceptibility of virtual presence reinforces the sense of social presence.[9] The 3D web is a *space of proximity*.

The perceptibility of virtual presence has immediate consequences for *accountability*. In the 2D web internet users are not directly accountable, because they are not directly visible and recognizable – except on communicative web

5. People first have to take a good look around in this 3D space, learn how to move around and how to communicate with other people. It takes a while to get used to this new world. You see newcomers in strange bodies taking their first unsteady steps in a strange environment. They stop to marvel at all the extraordinary creatures with peculiar names. The first experience with SL can best be compared to entering a pub where everybody is a stranger.

6. In pre-modern societies, space was the area in which one moved and time was the experience one had while moving through this space. In modern societies, social space is no longer restricted by predetermined spatial boundaries. We can now envision spaces we have never visited.

7. SL is not a separate environment unrelated to the internet. It is an integral part of the internet. Like e-mail, chatrooms and instant messaging, SL facilitates online communication. The possibilities of this communication and its media resources, however, are far greater than they were in Web 1.0.

8. The fewer communication channels available (e.g., only audio versus audio plus video), the more limited the capacity of the medium and the smaller its ability to deal with uncertainty and ambiguity. Owing to technological mediation, virtual teams and organizations are restricted in their ability to perform tasks with the greatest complexity and ambiguity. I have analysed this phenomenon in more detail in *Virtuele Organisatie en Communicatie*. See: www.sociosite.org/organisatie.php.

9. It has often been assumed that physical proximity is required for the realization of 'real' social relations and communities. In the classic formulation of Erving Goffmann, this condition of 'copresence' is stated as follows: 'Persons must sense that they are close enough to be perceived in whatever they are doing, including their experiencing of others, and close enough to be perceived in this sensing of being perceived' (Erving Goffmann, *Behavior in Public Places*, 1963:17). Now we know that personal relations and community formation can also occur in virtual arrangements when the *sense of social presence* can be generated there.

locations. In the 3D web, avatars present in the same location instantly experience one another's presence, recognize one another's virtual *identity* and can address one another directly.[10] This may lead to an improvement of opportunities for online self regulation; it's certainly a topic that calls for more research.[11]

Theoretically, possibilities for *expansion* of the 2D web are unlimited. In a practical sense, the number of sites is restricted only by the number of local servers that we can dispose of. This was and is the consequence of the decentralized character of the network of networks that forms the internet. For 3D environments such as SL, it has been a different matter so far. At the moment, organizing a private SL server and modelling the system on personal goals is still impossible. Thus the expansion of SL remains dependent on the number of central servers that make this internet environment run. SL is a *centralized network*. In such a network a central server ('broker') regulates traffic among individually registered users (à la Napster). Such a centralized architecture

10. As the use of virtual reality becomes more and more of an everyday activity, the boundary between physical and virtual space increasingly blurs. In the long run, virtual reality will become 'a low-resolution version of reality' (Mitchell Kapor). The virtual world is becoming a normal condition of our daily existence. Many SL participants are already experiencing a blurring of the boundary between their digitally constructed identity/identities and their appearance in local reality. They do not experience this as a problem, however, but as a challenge. They do not really care if the interactions that influence them come from the local or the virtual world. Most are highly aware of the fact that in cultivating their online personalities in SL they are also transforming themselves – perhaps completely.

11. The sustainability of one's existence and safety in SL depends on the extent to which participants collectively succeed in regulating the activities in SL and in protecting their community against criminal usurpations and commercial colonization. This capacity for self-regulation is no doubt the major success factor, as well as the major fail factor.

indeed facilitates efficient and extensive searching, but the system has only one entrance point. As a consequence, the network may collapse completely when one or more servers are put out of action.

This brings us to the last point of comparison: *power formation*. In the decentralized structure of the flat web the power of a site is determined by the number of visitors ('number of eyeballs'), the number of links that refer to a site and the reputation of these incoming links.[12] In the 3D space that is SL we are dealing with another type of power formation. Power in SL is realized in the form of the concentrated presence of

12. This has been described in more detail in my analysis of the topology and dynamics of the internet: *Zichzelf organiserende netwerken* (Self-organizing networks). See: www.sociosite.org/netwerken_theorie.php.

sites on a 'sim' (a spatially delineated part of the virtual space facilitated by Linden Lab). As a result, real power is usurped by sim administrators and property developers who operate as true colonizers of these virtual spaces.

Rights for SL-Citizens

We have seen that the 3D world of SL entails a series of transformations that can be compared to activities on the familiar flat web. These transformations have made the internet even more exciting and vital than it already was. Without a doubt, the most striking transformation lies in the field of the social presence that can be simulated in 3D environments. Criticism starts where the technology of SL is centralized (and privatized) in such a way that a premium is put on the power of capital, endangering the democratic standard of the virtual world.

SL is an extremely flexible and creative virtual world. It has had a strong evolution, has gained a worldwide reputation, and currently houses millions of enthusiastic residents. Yet SL is not without question the only and the best virtual world. Since the beginning of this century the number of virtual worlds has grown explosively. SL has to prove that it is robust enough to be accepted as a developing standard for the construction of a worldwide, 3D, multimedia virtual world. SL can prove this only by continuing to innovate rapidly. And even more than new technologies facilitated by SL, innovation depends on the creative energies of the residents of this virtual world. Furthermore, it is of the utmost importance that SL citizens obtain rights that can protect their carefully created digital constructions. Unfortunately, this is not yet the case.

David Garcia

The Politics
of Making

Effective Artistic Tools

Media researcher
and artist David
Garcia is dedicated
to achieving
effective media
tactics by artists
and internet
activists. Despite
the dominance
of the commer-
cial, absorbing
services industry
in which media
are pervasive,
Garcia believes that
they are nonethe-
less able to offer
ethical and critical
services by devel-
oping *tools*. He
discusses projects
by Bricolabs and
Mongrel, among
others.

The dilemma is simple and perhaps devastating: for decades artists and other critical media makers have laboured to bring about an ethos of mass participation in media making (the DIY media ethos) in the belief that challenging the centralized information monopolies would undermine the grip of corporate and state tyranny. But we are faced with the fact that though we are clearly witnessing the dawn of an era of mass participationn in media, the very opposite of a progressive agenda continues to dominate our world. We must face the possibility that a worst-case scenario has arisen in which by contributing to 'the big conversation', by becoming 'citizen journalists' by making 'tactical media' we may simply be victims of what political and media theorist Jodie Dean describes as 'communicative capitalism's perfect lure' in which 'subjects feel themselves to be active, even as their every action reinforces the status quo. Revelation can be allowed even celebrated and furthered because its results remain ineffectual.'[1]

1. Jodi Dean, 'Credibility and Certainty', paper delivered at a seminar in conjunction with the exhibition *Faith in Exposure*, Nederlands Media Art Institute-Montevideo/Time Based Arts, 24 February 2007.

I will engage with and counter this critique, with arguments illustrated through a number of case studies. It is my contention that these, along with many other examples, not only provide powerful alternatives to the dominant models of participation, but also help to demonstrate how impoverished and exploitative the dominant model of a participatory culture actually is. If we look beyond the projects circulat-

ing around the Web 2.0 hype, we can already find a wealth of impressive projects and communities of practice demonstrating that another world is indeed possible. But I will also argue that these progressive, practice-based initiatives must find ways to coordinate that generate far greater traction and impact. But before examining the ways in which this might happen we must begin by examining the dynamics behind the profound transformation that the media landscape has undergone since the emergence of the era of multimodal 'pervasive media' networks. (*Pervasive computing* is the trend in which more and more objects in our direct vicinity go on-line and communicate among themselves and with us - Ed.) No initiative can succeed without resonating effectively with this changed landscape.

Promises, Promises

As far back as 1996, the usually sober-minded political scientist Manuel Castells described in momentous terms what he believed to be happening. 'We are witnessing,' he declared, 'the formation of a hypertext and a meta-language which for the first time in history, integrate into the same system the written, oral and audio-visual modalities of human communication. . . . The human spirit reunites its dimensions in a new interaction between the two sides of the brain, machines and social contexts. For all the science-fiction ideology and commercial hype surrounding the so-called information superhighway, we can hardly underestimate its significance'.[2] The problem, however, was that at the time that Castells wrote these words, he (along with many commentators) was wildly overselling the internet as it then was. The grindingly slow dial-up connections of the pre-broadband era could not even begin to match the inflationary narratives of the 1990s. Indeed, at least part of the dotcom crash and subsequent 'tech winter' can be attributed to the disappointments of the actual experience delivered compared to the expectations generated by this kind of boosterism.

2. Manuel Castells, *The Information Age: Economy, Society, and Culture. Volume 1 – The Rise of the Network Society* (London: Blackwell, 1996), 328.

But a decade later the internet has started to deliver on a scale that brings the danger that today's critical commentators might make the opposite mistake. The default setting of 'knowing scepticism' in the face of any hint of inflationary claims can too easily prevent us from noticing when something really momentous is happening right under our noses. And this is the case now, as an ever-widening broadband rolls out and vastly improved compression rates mean that the premature claims made by the tech boosters of the 1990s are being repaid with interest. Not only has the multimodal communications universe described by Castells come to pass, but the modalities have also expanded to include 'touch' as we enter the era of the touch screen and thus of *tangible* pervasive media. The concept of the 'media landscape' has been transformed into something far more complex and multidimensional, what might be called a 'media ecology'. A new generation of mobile devices has meant that media have become ambient, rhizomatous, prosthetic; like Elvis, the media have left the building.

The Service Model

This era of pervasive media includes, but also takes us beyond either the Web 2.0 hype of user-generated content or even multimodality. It is sometimes called the 'internet of things'. In this multidimensional space, where the tangible and intangible are entwined, no device or website exists in isolation; all artefacts exist as part of a system or a network. To be successful, every device must become an interface to a 'service'. This fact has given rise to a new level of dominance for a particular industrial paradigm, the 'service industry'. The social relationships emphasized in service industries differ from the traditional marketplace in one crucial respect: while the typical market relationship is 'episodic, formed only for the purpose of a well-specified transfer of goods and resources and ending after that transfer',[3] the service model is entirely dependant on sustaining long-term and highly responsive relationships with their consumers.

3. Joe Podolny and Karen Page, 'Network Forms of Organisation', quoted in Felix Stalder, *Manuel Castells* (Key Contemporary Thinkers) (London: Polity, 2006), 177.

All aspects of production and social organization, from government downwards, are reorganizing themselves around this model of service provision. The service industry model puts the consumer – in this industrial discourse everyone is constructed as a consumer – at the centre, and we even hear talk of the era of consumer lead design. Many media artists and tactical-media activists would prefer to ignore the dominance of this powerful paradigm or dismiss it as a new kind of commodity fetishism, but to underestimate the seductions and also the real values embedded within the service model condemns oppositional practice to the margins. I will argue that critical engagement with the underlying dynamics of this new media ecology is essential to make critical practice more pertinent. Beginning with *Cool Media Hot Talk Show*, we will look at a number of exemplary projects by artists and media activists who in different ways are reshaping their practice to resonate more forcefully with the multimodal, service-orientated spaces we inhabit.

Revealing Antagonisms

Quietly, below the cultural radar, with a minimum fanfare, a remarkable tactical media development has been progressing at De Balie Centre for Culture and Politics in Amsterdam. In this remarkable organization, a top-notch team of ad-hoc developers, including Mauz Zero, Gerbrand Oudernaarden, Erik Kluitenburg and Michiel van der Haagen, Reza Tahmai, and Jeroen Joosse, have been rethinking the possibilities of archiving audiovisual content. Working with MMBase, an open-source content management and database tool developed by the Dutch broadcaster VPRO, the Balie media team has been using the opportunities offered by De Balie's infrastructure to web-cast its live events to develop experimental hybrid

media services. And to-date the most adventurous of these new Balie hybrids is the *Cool Media Hot talk Show* project (http://www.coolmediahottalk.net/), initiated by media-art scholar Tatiana Goryucheva.

At its most basic, the *Cool Media Hot Talk Show* is a real-time, interactive multimedia channel for art and media theory. Or, in Goryucheva's own words: 'A series of DIY interactive talk shows, where the public proposes and selects the topics, speakers, questions, and determines the final scenarios of the show.'[4] The project seeks to reflexively embody in its own structure the advanced questions it seeks to raise.

4. Tania Goryucheva's announcement on the *Spectre* mailing list, 21 March 2007.

Fully experiencing the *Cool Media Hot Talk Show* means engaging with the project on a number of levels. Firstly, the website is an interface to the live events in which artists and thinkers do short presentations at De Balie to a live audience and, of course, to the on-line public as well. But this is not simply a case of live lectures being screened through a website. The essence of the project depends on the public engaging with the speakers by putting questions to them through the website, either in advance or in a real-time response to the live talk. The questions are 'read out' (in order of popularity) by a digital simulation of a female voice. The speakers respond to each question in a set time of a couple of minutes, after which they are interrupted by this 'cyborg' moderator and must go on to the next question.

The results are occasionally humor-

Cool Media Hot Talk Show, orchestrated by Tatiana Goryucheva, www.coolmediahottalk.net.

ous and frequently clumsy, but the comic-book style of the interface (dominated by an eye-catching montage of a leggy cyborg in hot pants) is quite a strong hint that we are not supposed to take things all too seriously. Particularly amusing have been the rebellious speakers who find ways to subvert the *Cool Media Hot Talk Show* system. One of the more memorable was when artist and writer Armin Medosch rebelled against being asked questions by a 'machine' and responded with his own random selection of recordings. However, by refusing to answer questions from a so-called machine he also missed the point. It was not the machine that was asking the questions but people; the machine is simply mediating.

The apparent defects of *Cool Media Hot Talk Show* are inseparable from its qualities. Every glitch poses a new question for those exploring the different issues at stake when we try to develop alternative spaces for discourse. Above all, the project problematizes the power position of the traditional moderator, the power of the one who holds the microphone or the pen at the whiteboard, the disguised filtering techniques that are routinely deployed by human moderators, privileging some speakers and questions above others. Clearly stating rules and rigorously automating their implementation in this way does not provide answers to these power questions, nor does it pretend to; but by clarifying the protocols it holds up a lens enabling us to see, in sharpened relief, something of what is at stake in public discourse.

Both public debate and interactive multimedia products are frequently judged a success if they can be said to create 'flow'. A host of terms have been generated in the industrial sector to express the value of smoothly integrated and apparently effortless connection between elements in any system, terms such as seamlessness, friction-free media and blended media. One of the values of the *Cool Media Hot Talk Show* is precisely that it does not flow: it is an experiment that flies in the face of the requirement to be seamless. Neither its use of media nor its framing of discourse are in any sense 'blended'; rather, it proposes an aesthetics of juxtaposition which allows for maximum friction, dramatizing differences and amplifying the structural antagonism attendant on all genuine pluralism. Unlike the classical Web 2.0 spaces, the domains of user-generated content and social networking, the *Cool Media Hot Talk Show* is not for everyone; it is for 'anyone'.[5]

5. Adapted from Jeff Wall's poster statement: 'Art is Not for Everyone, It is for Anyone', 2006.

Multimodality and its possibilities for expanded forms of expressive discourse is one important dimension of an enhanced internet. But there is a second and the even more powerful property emerging: the advent of pervasive or ubiquitous media.

Service Design

The advent of pervasive media has fatally undermined the Cartesian divide between the tangible and intangible domains of production. The once-airy realm of media becomes ever more *tangible* as a new generation of tactile 'mobile devices' have propelled into prominence a new aesthetic of multiple 'touch-points'. We no longer think in terms of isolated artefacts or gadgets but of devices, and devices are above all interfaces to services. It is no longer possible to categorize the service industry as a sector apart. It has become the organizing paradigm for all industries, and is increasingly expressing itself through the important but deceptively banal-sounding discipline of 'service design'.

Service design is a critically positioned meta-discipline, orchestrating the domains of interaction design, product design, industrial engineering, consumer research and marketing. 'The need for a new category stems from the fact that production in a modern economy can no longer be seen in terms of the creation of isolated devices or websites, rather they exist as a system of tangible and intangible elements that together make up the service design experience. The by-now classic example of service design is the iPod with the iTunes software and the iTunes music online store. The overall service consists of tangible and intangible elements woven together to allow consumers to feel they are being offered the maximum in flexibility.'[6]

6. Geke van Dijk, in: David Garcia, et al. (eds.), *(Un)Common Ground: Creative Encounters Across Sectors and Disciplines* (Amsterdam: Bis, 2007), 29.

The perception (largely, but not entirely mythical) that the consumer is now in command has put the goal of creatively reshaping the relationship between producer and consumer at the heart of the new discipline of service design. This fact has lead to service design deploying increasingly sophisticated array of techniques and pedagogies that revolve around notions such as 'critical' or 'inclusive design'. These techniques have been developed, among others, at the Helen Hamlin Research Centre at London's Royal College of Art and at Goldsmiths College's Interaction Research programme (University of London). They borrow heavily from the 'subject centred' research methods pioneered by ethnographic filmmakers and anthropologists. In the product design world, these practices often take the form of 'domestic probes' and 'design documentaries'. These methods provide inspiration and insight for designers based on techniques that create empathy through enhanced forms of dialogue and even partnerships with consumers. These practices have become something of an orthodoxy and are widely seen in the design community as being more effective than earlier techniques of market research based on surveys and focus groups, which tend to objectify consumers.

A recent example is the project *Cultures of Mobility*,[7] in which Goldsmiths College and France Telecom collaborated to investigate the lives of people working away from home for extended periods of time. The study focused on students from Eastern European countries who came to the UK as summer fruit-pickers. Every year for up to six months they become inhabitants of transient communities. For the probe study, some

7. See http://www.goldsmiths.ac.uk/interaction/mobility.html.

of these student-workers were given materials to complete and customize, to give the design team a feel for their home lives away from home. 'In combination with a design documentary and the continuation of the study in the homeland of the participants,' it was claimed by the researchers, the results provided 'a rich and inspiring mix of research data was gathered'.[8]   8. Van Dijk, op. cit. (note 6), 32.

Radical practitioners might argue that it is wrong to treat that most exploited and marginalized of groups – migrant labour – as a subject for an exercise in market research. But Bas Raijmakers (one of the researchers involved) stoutly defends the project from these attacks, declaring that those who watched the documentary were soon revising their assumptions. Those who viewed the film did not see a new class of victims, but rather students from Eastern Europe making what for them was good money, which would be used to create a better future for themselves in the new member countries of the EU. Raijmakers also argued that it is an inherently progressive position for a designer to be serving less well-off members of society.

Activist Makers

Political activists may do their work through networks of protest, combining direct action with media and information politics. But increasingly, radical politics is also being carried out through networks of *production*, in which 'social techno hackers' collaborate in processes of 'open making'. We must define this new category of 'activist makers' carefully. It is not simply a question of the protocols used; it is also a matter of the guiding motive or intention. Activist makers are not those – and there are many – who simply deploy 'open-source' methods as an expedient way of getting things made or done. The activist maker's primary motive is to demonstrate (in practice) that another world, a world not founded on exploitation, is possible. This includes, but goes beyond, the drive for social and economic justice – all these laudable goals; activist makers are driven by the vision of freedom based on maximizing creative participation for all.

This way of doing politics has reached the kind of critical mass whereby we can realistically speak of a 'movement' of activist makers. Scale is no longer simply a background fact; it is *the* subject to be faced by activist makers, who need to learn how to collaborate more effectively across their differences if they are to better manage their transitions up and down the registers of scale.

In 2006, the Bricolabs project emerged as a way to address this need to 'scale up' through coordinating the tangible and intangible modes of activist making. It began as a 'collaborative exchange between Brazilian, Indonesian, UK, Chinese, Indian and Dutch open-source experts, building capacity and connections for existent groups of *bricoleurs*, public, private . . .'[9] In itself there is nothing very exceptional in   9. See the Bricolabs website: http://bricolabs.net/.

any of this; what sets Bricolabs apart is its attempt to address the issue of scale through seeking to break open and connect all aspects of making, hardware as well as software, content as well as networks. They call this approach 'full loop' development; this kind of development is the norm in the commercial sector, but the price of the success stories is the creation of inherently 'closed' systems, where the only choices are the ones that are prescribed. By contrast, the aspiration of Bricolabs is to create awareness and opportunities and to connect the different interpenetrating layers of content, applications/ services, operating systems, hardware, networks and so to shape a 'generic infrastructure' that is open and shared. Bricolabs is a valuable paradox, a space for developing strategies for remaining 'tactical'. It is, however, at an early stage of development, with a great deal still to prove. But there is one important collective of artist-activist makers, called Mongrel, which has been working for two decades, generating an inspiring collection of projects worthy of its own museum retrospective.

Mongrel's *Poor to Poor* Networks

Aesthetically and politically, nothing could be further from the antiseptic term 'service design' than the English artists' collective Mongrel. For more than two decades, Mongrel has been working on the frontline of street culture, art and media, not only in England but also as far afield as Jamaica and South Africa. The group's ability to collapse issues of techno-politics and class is encapsulated by the subtitle of one of their networking projects

(*Skint*), which they dubbed *Poor to Poor*. Aesthetically, Mongrel's output is a potent fusion of politically engaged DIY techno culture, whose aesthetic origins lay in the Fanzine culture of England's Punk movement of the late 1970s. Respected throughout the world, their antagonistic stance has had a price; in England at least they remain the perpetual outsiders. Mongrel is the very best of bloody-minded England.

Many of Mongrel's projects demonstrate in the most ethical and critical manner imaginable how artists can indeed produce work that provides a service. Mongrel's work is incredibly rich and varied. But for our purposes we will restrict ourselves to examining a small but significant part of their output, a series of projects they have dubbed 'social telephony'. This series of projects began in 2001 with *TextFM*, which involved turning text messages left on mobile phones into voice simulations which were then patched into local radio programmes. Since then they have developed a range of projects that combine phones, mobiles and free web-based calls with the flexibility of the internet. They use mobile technology to build networks between communities, which act as public interfaces for cultural projects. The latest and most developed example of their 'contagious' telephone-media projects is *Telephone Trottoire* (2006) (www.mongrel. org.uk/?q=trottoire), which follows the Mongrel philosophy of engaging communities who have fallen outside of the mainstream social networks.

Telephone Trottoire was a collaboration with the radio programme *Nostalgia Ya*

Mboka, which serves the over 35,000 Congolese living in London, over 90 per cent of whom are political refugees or asylum seekers. Unlike so many projects from the radical free-software community, Mongrel's social telephony projects do not rely on unfamiliar computer systems and only require phone connectivity.

The *trottoire* of the project's title is taken from the Congolese practice of *radio trottoire* (pavement radio), the circulation of news and gossip between individuals on street corners. Using cheap telephony cards and free software, *Telephone Trottoire* allowed people to build social networks, passing phone calls to one another through auto-dialling and allowing them to transmit content among themselves through their phones.

Unfortunately, the project lasted for just six weeks, but as a proof of concept the results were remarkable. According to Mongrel, their user-base grew at a rate of 10 per cent every day, resulting in a total of 448 individual recorded messages from locations across the UK, including London, Birmingham, Manchester and Liverpool, as well as internationally from as far afield as Ireland, Canada, Belgium, France, South Africa and of course DRC itself.[10]

10. Media Shed pamphlet, produced for Enter Unknown Territories Festival, Cambridge 2007.

Telephone Trottoire is inspiring but it also points to the limitations of many tactical media interventions. A commercially resourced service, for all its defects, might have been more likely to achieve a sustained relationship with its community of users. But it is not yet 'game over'. At the time of writing there are signs that Mongrel has plans to re-launch *Telephone Trottoire* on a larger scale.

Conclusion

It is time to return to our point of departure, to Jodie Dean's contention that the ideal of openness, upon which so much of the tactical media and activist making I have been describing are based, is 'not only ill-suited to a mass political age but is also part of the ideological apparatus that furthers the expansion of networked information technologies to consolidate communicative capitalism.'[11]

11. Dean, op. cit. (note 1).

Two years ago I put a similar argument to a group of pirate media activists in Brazil, who work in the *favelas* as educators creating free media spaces with pirate radio and other tools. 'No!' they objected. 'For us media is a vital battlefield, particularly in Latin America where monopolistic media giants like Brazil's Globo pump out an endless narcotic diet of soaps, game shows and football that help to keep poor people passive.' For these activists there can be no imaginable political strategy that does not involve the *expressive* dimension.

By an expressive dimension I am not only referring to 'cultural politics' in which an earlier generation of thinkers and artists addressed issues of 'representation'. An 'expressivist'[12] politics deploys the power of language in the broadest sense of

12. My use of the term 'expressivism' is taken from Charles Taylor's analysis of Herder's 'alternative anthropology, one centered

Telephone Trottoire (2006) is a Mongrel project, in cooperation with Nostalgia Ya Mboka.

the word, (including the visual, sonic and motoric languages from which the arts are constituted). Expressivism is based on our awareness that in a world of contingent horizons, our sense of meaning depends, critically, on our powers of expression. 'And that discovering a framework of meaning is interwoven with invention.'[13]

on categories of expression'. In a footnote in Taylor's *Hegel* (Cambridge: Cambridge University Press, 1975), 13, he describes how he and Isaiah Berlin decided on the term 'expressivism' in a private communication. Expressivism was prefered to 'expressionism' so as to to avoid confusion with the twentieth century art movement.

13. Charles Taylor, *Sources of the Self, The Making of the Modern Identity* (Cambridge: Cambridge University Press, 1989), 22.

This approach is captured by the Italian activist and autonomist thinker Franco Berardi 'Bifo', who wrote: 'What interests us in the image is not its function as representation of reality, but its dynamic potential, its capacity to elicit and construct projections, interactions, narrative frames . . . devices for constructing reality.'[14]

14. Franco Berardi 'Bifo', 'Limmagine dispositivo', quoted in Brian Holmes, 'Do-It-Yourself Geopolitics: Cartographies of Art in the World', in: Blake Simpson and Gregory Sholette (eds.), *Collectivism After Modernism. The Art of Social Imagination After 1945* (Minneapolis: University of Minnesota Press, 2007), 273.

But beyond Bifo's clarion call, the potential of new media does not lie in expression alone, but in *making*. New media are not just language channels; they are tool-making environments. Activist artists and makers are frequently toolmakers, committed to sharing their know-how; their most appropriate textual genre may not be the manifesto but the *manual*.

There is another argument to be made by those who would oppose those like Jodie Dean seeking to dismiss the ideal of openness as ideology. This argument champions openness as a protection against some of the more extreme forms of despotism that occur when we abandon a sceptical epistemology. This version of the ideal of openness is founded on the awareness that knowledge (even when armed with our most powerful knowledge-acquiring techniques) can only ever be partial. Žižek famously makes the distinction between 'knowing' and 'believing'. But in our world, 'neither knowing nor believing is enough. Claims have to be proven, every day, day after day, again and again. These are the constraints of politics in conditions of pluralism.'[15]

15. Noortje Marres, 'The Need (not) to Know: After New Media – Shifting Conditions for Democracy'. A review of J. Dean, *Publicity's Secret* (Ithaca/London: Cornell University Press, 2002) in: *Space and Culture* (2004) 7, 119-125.

column

HENRY JENKINS

NINE PROPOSITIONS TOWARDS
A CULTURAL THEORY OF YOUTUBE

1. YouTube represents the kind of hybrid media space described by Yochai Benkler in *The Wealth of Networks* – a space where commercial, amateur, non-profit, governmental, educational and activist content coexists and interacts in ever more complex ways. As such, it potentially represents a site of conflict and renegotiation between different forms of power. One interesting illustration of this is the emergence of Astroturf – fake grassroots media – through which very powerful groups attempt to mask themselves as powerless in order to gain greater credibility within participatory culture. In the past, these powerful interests would have been content to exert their control over broadcast and mass-market media, but now they often have to mask their power in order to operate within network culture.

2. YouTube has emerged as the meeting point between a range of different grassroots communities involved in the production and circulation of media content. Much that is written about YouTube implies that the availability of Web 2.0 technologies has enabled the growth of participatory cultures. I would argue the opposite: that it was the emergence of participatory cultures of all kinds over the past several decades that has paved the way for the early embrace, quick adoption and diverse use of platforms like YouTube. But as these various fan communities, brand communities and subcultures come together through this common portal, they are learning techniques and practices from each other, accelerating innovation within and across these different communities of practice. One might well ask whether the 'You' in YouTube is singular or plural, given the fact that the same word functions for both in the English language. Is YouTube a site for personal expression, as is often claimed in news coverage, or for the expression of shared visions within common communities? I would argue that the most powerful content on YouTube comes from and is taken up by specific communities of practice and is thus in that sense a form of cultural collaboration.

3. YouTube represents a site where amateur curators assess the value of commercial content and re-present it for various niche communities of consumers. YouTube participants respond to the endless flow and multiple channels of mass media by making selections, choosing meaningful

moments which then get added to a shared archive. Increasingly, we are finding clips that gain greater visibility through YouTube than they achieved via the broadcast and cable channels from which they originated. A classic example of this might be the entertainer/writer Colbert appearance at the Washington Press Club Dinner. The media companies are uncertain how to deal with the curatorial functions of YouTube: seeing it as a form of viral marketing on some occasions and a threat to their control over their intellectual property on others. We can see this when Colbert and his staff encourage fans to remix his content the same week that the media conglomerate Viacom seeks legal action to have Colbert clips removed from YouTube.

4. YouTube's value depends heavily upon its deployment via other social networking sites — with content gaining much greater visibility and circulation when promoted via blogs, Live Journal, MySpace and the like. While some people come and surf YouTube, its real breakthrough came in making it easy for people to spread its content across the web. In that regard, YouTube represents a shift away from an era of stickyness (where the goal was to attract and hold spectators on your site, like a roach motel) and towards an era where the highest value is in spreadability (a term which emphasizes the active agency of consumers in creating value and heightening

awareness through their circulation of media content).

5. YouTube operates, alongside Flickr, as an important site for citizen journalists, taking advantage of a world where most people have cameras embedded in their cell phones which they carry with them everywhere they go. We can see many examples of stories or images in the past year which would not have gotten media attention if someone hadn't thought to record them as they unfolded using readily accessible recording equipment: George Allen's 'macaca' comments, the tazering incident in the UCLA library, Michael Richards's racist outburst in the nightclub, even the footage of Sadam Hussein's execution, are a product of this powerful mixture of mobile technology and digital distribution.

6. YouTube may embody a particular opportunity for translating participatory culture into civic engagement. The ways that Apple's '1984' advertisement was appropriated and deployed by supporters of Obama and Clinton as part of the political debate suggests how central YouTube may become in the next presidential campaign. In many ways, YouTube may best embody the vision of a more popular political culture that Stephen Duncombe discusses in his new book, *Dream: Re-Imagining Progressive Politics in the Age of Fantasy*: 'Progressives should have learned to build a politics that embraces

the dreams of people and fashions spectacles which gives these fantasies form – a politics that employs symbols and associations, a politics that tells good stories. In brief, we should have learned to manufacture dissent. . . . Given the progressive ideals of egalitarianism and a politics that values the input of everyone, our dreamscapes will not be created by media-savvy experts of the left and then handed down to the rest of us to watch, consume, and believe. Instead, our spectacles will be participatory: dreams that the public can mold and shape themselves. They will be active: spectacles that work only if the people help create them. They will be open-ended: setting stages to ask questions and leaving silences to formulate answers. And they will be transparent: dreams that one knows are dreams but which still have power to attract and inspire. And, finally, the spectacles we create will not cover over or replace reality and truth but perform and amplify it.'

Yet as we do so, we should also recognize that participatory culture is not always progressive. However low they may set the bar, the existing political parties do set limits on what they will say in the heat of the political debate and we should anticipate waves of racism, sexism and other forms of bigotry as a general public, operating outside of those rules and norms, deploy participatory media to respond to a race which includes women, Afri-can-Americans, Hispanics, Mormons, Italian-Americans, Catholics, and the like as leading figures in a struggle for control over the White House.

7. YouTube helps us to see the shifts which are occurring in the cultural economy: the grassroots culture appropriates and remixes content from the mass-media industry; the mass-media industry monitors trends and pulls innovations back into the system, amplifying them and spreading them to other populations. Yet as they do so, they often alter the social and economic relations which fuelled this cultural production in the first place. We will see increasing debates about the relations between the gift economy of participatory culture and the commodity relations that characterize user-generated content. There is certainly a way that these sites can be seen as a way of economic exploitation as they outsource media production from highly paid and specialized creative workers to their amateur unpaid counterparts.

8. In the age of YouTube, social networking emerges as one of the important social skills and cultural competencies that young people need to acquire if they are going to become meaningful participants in the culture around them. We need to be concerned with the participation gap as much as we are concerned with the digital divide. The digital divide has to do with access to tech-

nology; the participation gap has to do with access to cultural experiences and the skills that people acquire through their participation within ongoing online communities and social networks.

9. YouTube teaches us that a participatory culture is not necessarily a diverse culture. As John McMuria has shown us, minorities are grossly under-represented – at least among the most heavily viewed videos on YouTube, which still tend to come most often from white middle-class males. If we want to see a more 'democratic' culture, we need to explore what mechanisms might encouraged greater diversity in who participates, whose work gets seen, and what gets valued within the new participatory culture.

This text was taken from Henry Jenkins' weblog: www.henryjenkins.org, 28 May 2007.

Willem van Weelden

Wading in the Info Sea

An Interview with Richard Rogers about Web Epistemology and Information Politics

How can the web be understood as both a symptom and an expression of a public practice? According to what logic do search engines work and how do they influence the way we deal with knowledge, news and information? Web epistemology is a new research practice that regards the web as a separate knowledge culture and advocates giving an ear to what lies beyond all the din. An interview with Richard Rogers, web epistemologist at the University of Amsterdam, author of *Information Politics on the Web*, founder of the Govcom.org Foundation and developer of the Issue Crawler, an 'info-political tool'.[1]

1. For information about projects like the *Issue Crawler* and about publications by Richard Rogers, see http:/ www.govcom.org.

The very beginning of the information revolution was described by the philosopher Jean-François Lyotard as something that instils an inherent anxiety: the fear that scientific knowledge would become a commodity like all information, which would thus drastically alter the status of knowledge.[2] He proposed that knowledge would no longer be disseminated for its 'formative' value, but in the framework of daily maintenance. Knowledge ceases to be an aim in itself; it loses

2. Jean-François Lyotard, *La condition postmoderne: rapport sur le savoir* (Paris: Minuit, 1979).

its 'use-value' and becomes a commercial commodity circulated along the same channels and networks as money. The distinction would no longer be between knowledge and ignorance, but between payment knowledge and investment knowledge. (According to the dominant liberal ideology, some flows of money are used in decision making, while others are only good for payments.)

This immediately raises the issue of 'access': who will have access to knowledge and under what conditions, and who will decide which channels are forbidden? In this social conflict Lyotard saw no decisive role either for the state or for knowledge. In the postmodern analysis, after all, the state is no longer the governing factor of social and political life. Power is no longer exercised on the basis of ideological contrasts or grand narratives, but is dictated by economic movements. What's more, the same analysis shows that science is caught up in an internal crisis: any formulated knowledge has to ultimately acquire its legitimacy in another knowledge. The economy, and hence social life, is henceforth dependent for its dynamism and 'development' on social agencies that not only control access to the information society, but also provide the networks that shape this society.

At the beginning of the 1980s Lyotard outlined a technocratic spectre, suggesting that the crisis of knowledge lies in its historical origins. At the same time, he distilled from the diagnosis of this crisis a programme of what was at stake in thinking, philosophy, science and the arts: the restoration of the honour of thinking and knowing by critically investigating the new technocratic conditions under which it exists. The 'conditional' approach he chose for this was based in part on systems theory. Society is only really a system when the relations that constitute it are optimalized as regards performativity and efficiency.

This means that the critical tradition, including philosophy, art and science, is in danger of being systematically co-opted in order to strengthen the technocratic whole, even though it has a different agenda. The only way to escape from this 'paranoia of Reason' is through a deeply rooted distrust as regards all forms of appropriation. The crucial question continues to be how critique can be practised when the critical agency itself is also an instrument that is part of the whole it is attempting to describe.

During the last decade, search engines have drastically changed the way we regard knowledge. The use of clever algorithms for search queries accommodates the vast amount of information offered by the internet and meets the wishes of the millions of internet surfers who consult the web for their daily information needs and production. Search engines are also more than advisory systems that indicate in a quasi neutral manner what information is available on the internet; they are also suppliers of semi-finished knowledge that is supplemented and changed so as to become new information which in many cases is then published again on the internet. Search engines have not only intervened deeply in how we interact with the internet, but the way we deal with and produce knowledge and how access to it is gained have also radically changed. For the internet is not organized like a library; search engines clearly utilize a different logic than library systems based on thesauri and lexical indexing. The modernist endeavour to preclude interpretation has mutated in postmodern reality into an elegant, critical surfing of interpretations, where improbabilities are welcome. Search engines are now looking for users – not the other way around.

Since the enthusiastic beginning of the web, the 'web spirit' has been dominated by the expectation that this new public domain would be egalitarian and democratic. The chaos, anarchy or lack of organization that this entailed was seen as a positive quality. The web was regarded as a corrective to the offline world. The web site of a private individual was just as visible as that of a big company. Domain names often did not correspond with their offline variants. McDonalds.com, for example, belonged to a private individual who had nothing to do with the hamburger concern. These were the times before search engines, portals, web browsers and selective hyperlinking would start to determine the face of the web.

The advent of search engines in the second half of the 1990s (Webcrawler, AltaVista, Yahoo) revealed the changed status of information or knowledge in an insistent way. The 'preferred placement case' (1998) serves as a good illustration of this. AltaVista, then the most respected search engine, decided to sell the first two links (known as 'pole positions') resulting from a search. This gave rise to the difference between purchased results and organic results, the 'neutral' results generated by search engines with the help of algorithms, but without that difference being visible to users. This 'preferred listing' led to vehement criticism from 'freedom fighters' who called for an end to this 'advertorial' practice. The neutrality of the algorithms with which the search engines worked was not to be besmirched by commercial interference. After a few months the practice was abandoned, but all the commotion had damaged AltaVista's reputation and it lost its position of power.

The controversy created by the preferred placement case was not only relevant for studying the effects of preconfigured networks and media technology, but also raised the issue of the aim of the web itself. The preferred placement case led the Amsterdam-based American researcher Richard Rogers to concentrate on what he calls web epistemology: an empirical study concentrated in the research group he founded under the name govcom.org, which investigates the web precisely at the point of intersection between medium and user. Web epistemology is concerned with what the web knows, how it knows that and why certain sources are chosen above others. At the forefront are issues concerning the authenticity of sources, the algorithms with which search engines work and the functioning of the internet as the whole of its users and technology. In short, research focussing on 'Knowledge Politics on the Web', the subtitle to the 2000 book that Rogers devoted to the Preferred Placement project.[3]

3. Richard Rogers (ed.), *Preferred Placement: Knowledge Politics on the Web* (Maastricht/Amsterdam: Jan van Eyck Akademie Editions/de Balie, 2000).

Willem van Weelden: *What insight led you to web epistemology?*

Richard Rogers: What we are looking at in the contemporary period, whether it's through the rise of the amateur or through the rise of search engines, tools and algorithms that take the amateur more seriously, is the redistribution of attention. It's very difficult for a lot of people to think about the consequences of new media, because there are a number of things that people tend to fall back on, like 'the good journalist', in the assumption that the web is a rumour mill, or the blogosphere an 'echo chamber'. If you're working with these types of assumptions you are already thinking epistemologically. The natural impulse of the traditional journalist, or even the digital journalist, would be to trace a story back to its source. But in the new media way of thinking, the way it is built in in Google News for example, the scoop or the original source is not rewarded. The original source is buried; what is shown is the circulation and what is the freshest. From a journalistic standpoint it is too fresh to be true! From a web-epistemological point of view the question is why the most recent source should be rewarded. It is about first of all identifying the differences between what is considered to be relevant, important or significant in the old approach versus this new way of thinking.

This insight is the start of what you could call a web epistemology. What we've been doing in a number of our projects is to study how this redistribution of attention is captured. It is no surprise that a development like the rise of the amateur is connected to the web.

In the past the web already disrupted how we decide on what matters. The next step is to ask yourself the question: 'How do you study how this manifests itself?' First you look at what sort of data streams are available to the makers of the search engines. For Google it was a major breakthrough, in a certain sense already an original Web 2.0 thought, when they formulated algorithms on the basis of 'we are not going to rely on what individuals say about something, we are going to rely on what others say'. They argued: 'We are going to count links, and if the site has a lot of links it must be very relevant, and if the link in its pointer text has the word that matches the query, then the site that has the most links with the correct pointer text is the one that ends up at the top.[4] No experts, no authorities determine the ranking!' Their way of thinking is very much concentrated on: 'What are the data streams or data sources that we have, how can we organize them and, finally, how can we recommend that information?' They just use what's available to them. How many links? They use date stamps: how fresh is it? Once one identifies all of these potential things that you can use to count and to put into algorithms then you can ultimately recommend, putting one source on top of another source. So we must no longer rely on what individuals say about their own importance (self appointing), nor on what independent experts say is important; it's mainly a question of where sites refer to with their most recent links. And if you let that thought sink in you begin to realize the massive reverberation that has.

4. The *pointer text* is the text that can be clicked on [editor's note].

What was the 'drama' you found in the Preferred Placement project and why was that so important for your research?

It is very much a matter of de-equalization. In the Jan van Eyck period[5] we also talked about the web in terms completely opposite to those used at the time. We were against this 'public sphere' or that idea of 'equality', as if such notions were incorporated into the infrastructure of the web.[6] We were looking for public debate and we found something different. We found issue networks, through empirical research. We were looking for some sort of evidence of this neo-pluralistic space, where there was some sort of flat ontology, where sources were next to each other, the side-by-sideness principle. The Whole Earth Catalogue in 1994 already showed that the eminent expert and the crackpot are side by side. That's a very interesting thing, and a very important feature of the web.[7] Side-by-sideness, however, is gradually disappearing. By ranking sites, search engines create hierarchies of credibility and these can differ from traditional, pre-web methods for determining credibility or reliable sources. This is exactly what the study of web epistemology is about.

5. The book *Preferred Placement: Knowledge Politics on the Web* emerged from research at the Jan van Eyck Academy in Maastricht, 1999-2000 [editor's note].

6. See also Noortje Marres, *No Issue, No Public: Democratic Deficits after the Displacement of Politics* (Amsterdam: Universiteit van Amsterdam, 2005), dissertation.

7. Howard Rheingold, *The Millennium Whole Earth Catalog* (Harper, 1994), 263. 'The least discussed, but most important aspect of what's ahead is quality assurance. The democratic nature of the Net, where eminent scientists and isolated crackpots can publish side by side, leads to wide variations in the self policing . . . Authenticating that a resource is the definitive, unedited version is next to impossible.'

The 'Preferred Placement' study was very much about the drama of search engines. As you know, the term 'PP' was coined by AltaVista as an advertising service: you could buy preferred placement so that your site would be at the top of the list for certain queries. You can think of this rather mundanely as yet another advertising service – 'we've found new ad space' – but to us it was more about the perceived importance of being at the top of an authoritative space, whose authority supposedly derived from a 'neutral' algorithm, for in the search engine industry results that are not paid for are called 'organic'. On the one hand we tried to critique this 'neutrality' of search engine results, and on the other hand we wanted to deal with the 'drama' in that space. The idea that as a company or organization you need to be at the top, and then you are faced with the drama of being driven out of the first ranks. The daily quest to find out where you are today in the list: 'Oops, I've sunk four places', or the drama of being dropped from the top ten!

Most recently, and that was a sort of dream of mine, we created a tool that is called the 'Issue Dramaturg' (http://issuedramaturg.issuecrawler.net/) which shows over time a site's page rank for a particular query. If you put the query 'climate change' or 'RFID' into a search engine then the results somehow influence your view of the world. You don't often pose yourself the question as to whether this particular organization is researching RFID, for I don't see them here, so where are they, and how are they doing? And where is *spychips.com* when I type in the query 'RFID'? How are they doing? So with the *Issue Dramaturg* we make this drama visible. This project started with the *Preferred Placement* project, purely to investigate page ranking. Just type in 'http' or 'www' and what you get is basically the top of the net. Then we spent a while looking at what was at the top and we saw that the *New York Times*, for example, climbed from 76th to 12th place over a period of three months. Later, with Dragana Antic, a student at the Piet Zwart Academy, we showed how this 'Hyperlink Economy' works.[8]

8. See http://www.govcom.org/maps/ map_set_wsis/GC0_Maps_set_3.0_ link_economy_1_2_v2.pdf.

The problem with the sort of research you are doing is that you are bound up with what you are investigating. You're using search engines to examine how they work. How can you escape from this 'paranoia of Reason'?

With the notion of info politics. Epistemologies have consequences. First we have to recognize that there are several epistemologies. Directories are made in a different way than search engines. And they have different assumptions about which sources should be counted. In the late 1990s the question was always what the value of information was. And our question has always been not what counts as much as who decides what counts? And then once you have thought that through a little then you test the outcomes infopolitically. *Information Politics on the Web* starts with the important consideration that information

An analysis of the geographical distribution of blogging by issue on globalvoicesonline.org.

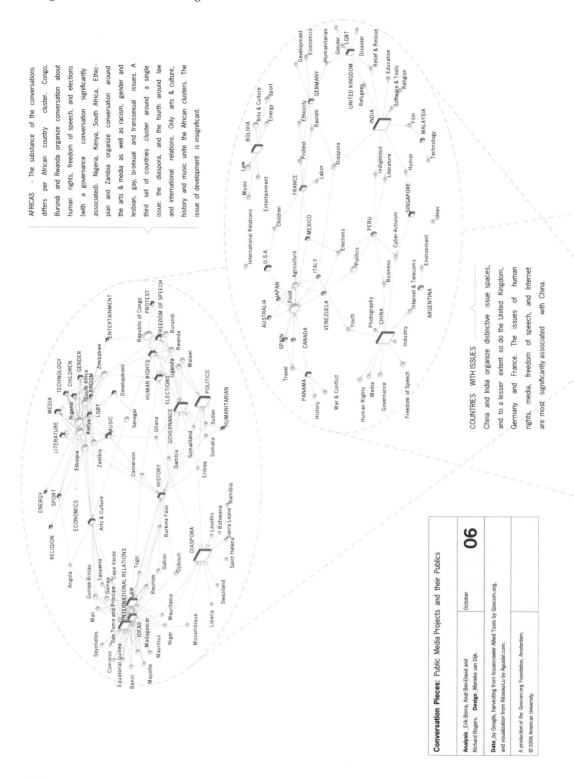

AFRICAS - The substance of the conversations differs per African country cluster. Congo, Burundi and Rwanda organize conversation about human rights, freedom of speech, and elections (with a governance conversation significantly associated). Nigeria, Kenya, South Africa, Ethiopian and Zambia organize conversation around the arts & media as well as racism, gender and lesbian, gay, bi-sexual and transsexual issues. A third set of countries cluster around a single issue: the diaspora, and the fourth around law and international relations. Only arts & culture, history and music unite the African clusters. The issue of development is insignificant.

COUNTRIES WITH ISSUES —— China and India organize distinctive issue spaces, and to a lesser extent so do the United Kingdom, Germany and France. The issues of human rights, media, freedom of speech, and Internet are most significantly associated with China.

Conversation Pieces: Public Media Projects and their Publics

October **06**

Analysis _ Erik Borra, Anat Ben-David and Richard Rogers. **Design** _ Marieke van Dijk.

Data _ by Google, harvesting from Issuecrawler Allied Tools by Govcom.org, and visualization from Réseau-Lu by Aguidel.com.

A production of the Govcom.org Foundation, Amsterdam.
© 2006 American University.

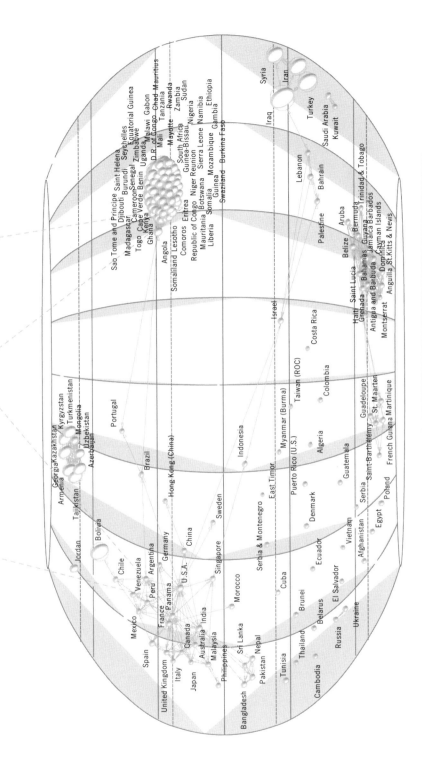

"Global Voices" cluster regionally. The main non-regional grouping is 'globalized' in the sense that it comprises G8 countries (+China). Inter-regional substantive conversation is insignificant.

* Bridge blogging? "Blogs designed to increase communication between people from different countries and cultures." Global Voices Online > FAQ, http://www.globalvoicesonline.org/? page_id=272

Legend (region-issue zoom maps)

Countries

Issues

Source: globalvoicesonline.org, 1 October 2005 - 1 October 2006.
Scrape at http://devel.issuecrawler.net/~erik/gvo/gvo/index.php .
Co-occurrence analysis of countries and issues.

has long been regarded as something a-political.[9] What the web has helped us to see again is that sources are in constant competition to be the source. Sources are dying to inform you! You have to think of algorithms politically, by testing the consequences of a particular algorithm.

9. Richard Rogers, *Information Politics on the Web* (Cambridge, MA: MIT Press, 2004).

But to come back to the idea of side-by-sideness as something to strive for, you have to imagine what I discovered in 2004 when I typed in 'terrorism'. I was interested in the question whether the algorithm would produce familiar hierarchies of credibility, familiar in the sense of what the TV news would bring, or would they show something else? I typed it in and the results were: CIA.gov, FBI.gov, Whitehouse.gov, Heritiage Foundation, and somewhere further down the list were CNN and Al Jazeera. You have to understand that the algorithm gives these sources the privilege of informing us about terrorism. Where is the 'side-by-sideness' in that list? Then you ask yourself: 'How do you solve this?' Well, by looking at the infopolitical consequences of your own practice.

Can you be more precise about that? What is such an infopolitical consequence?

The web makes us face the fact that there is a multiplicity of sources. The question we asked was: 'Is an issue hot because it is in the news?' What we did was to think in terms of how the web brings us beyond the notion of news. So we did the project infoid.org, where we took advantage of the web as a multiple source space.[10] What we also did was to look at another common idea that people have about the web, namely that it speeds things up

10. http://www.infoid.org.

and leads to journalistic sloppiness, because there seems to be no more time anymore. But by checking on the web empirically and looking at the difference between how the news covers certain issues and how issue professionals cover them, we discovered that issue professionals have a much longer attention span than the news to particular issues. It shows that with the web things aren't sped up; people have longer attention spans! The heat of an issue is no longer determined by the news. Generally speaking what we do is undertake research that would be impossible without the web.

Does your research show that in the way they relate to the news users have become more accustomed to this principle and that they use the internet more critically?

We do not study users! A very important thing to know is that we study what is published, not what is read! We identified and described this given in terms of the differences between the hit economy and the link economy. Once it was assumed that you could determine how much interest a site garnered by counting the number of hits, but nowadays it's a question of a link-economy, which is about pointers. We tried to develop new ways of describing webdynamics which are not necessarily familiar. What we are trying to do is in that respect uncomfortable.

Can you say something about how your research looks at specific terminology in order to arrive at an issue?

We rely on specific issue terminology and make use of that as a research technique. We used these techniques in the Election Issue Tracker, for example, by pulling out the specific issue language of, say, Lijst Pim Fortuyn (LPF) and comparing it to the language in the same general issue area of other parties. We ran batch queries nightly of all the newspapers and we watched how specific issue language was resonating in the press. And what we found was that, generally speaking, the press was using the language of the populist parties with greater frequency than the language of non-populist parties. So we were able to raise the question of to what extent the press was participating in the rise of populism. It showed that the newspaper's information is in some sense political.

In your research you make a methodological distinction between issue networks, social networks and stranger networks. Can you say something about this in relation to more common forms of social research into the internet?

The distinction between different types of networks is one way to try to differentiate our work from the social network analysts. Social network analysts generally use surveys and questionnaires to determine ties between individuals, whereas what we do is study links in order to demonstrate what are essentially very normal strategies for establishing connections between organizations, and we do this on the basis of issues. These organizations do not necessarily have to work together or even be on good terms with each other; they might oppose each other or be enemies. And what we strive to locate is a different set of actors who are implicated in a certain issue area. I'm using these words so as to try to differentiate what a social network analyst would do. When you study the networks well, they not only reveal who are involved but also who is the addressee of the issue. Those who can be considered as the parties that are expected to contribute to the settlement of the issue. That's the difference. And the notion of stranger networks comes from thinking about social movements. What is the difference between a social movement and a network? A social movement often has an ideal demographic that is largely derived from the Paris '68 uprising, a classic constellation of students and workers. Another example is the peace movement in the 1980s around such issues as nuclear energy and

The Web Issue Index of Civil Society (Issue Ticker), with touch-screen, on display at the Zentrum für Kunst und Medientechnologien, Karlsruhe, Germany, 2005.

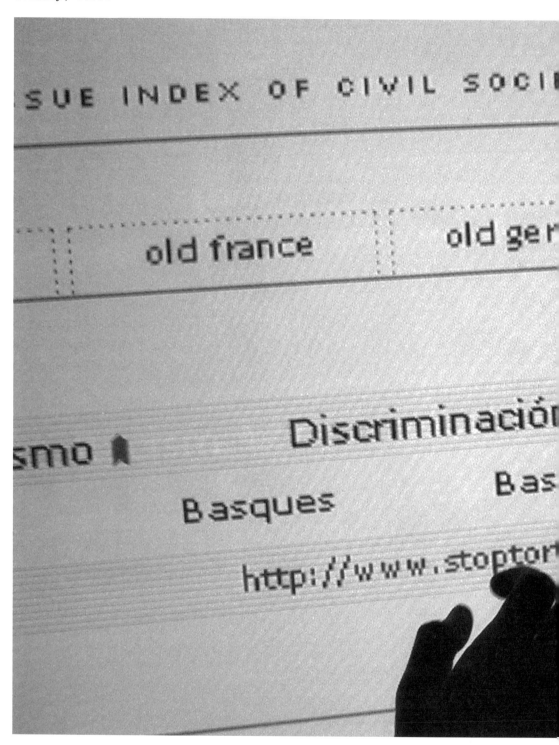

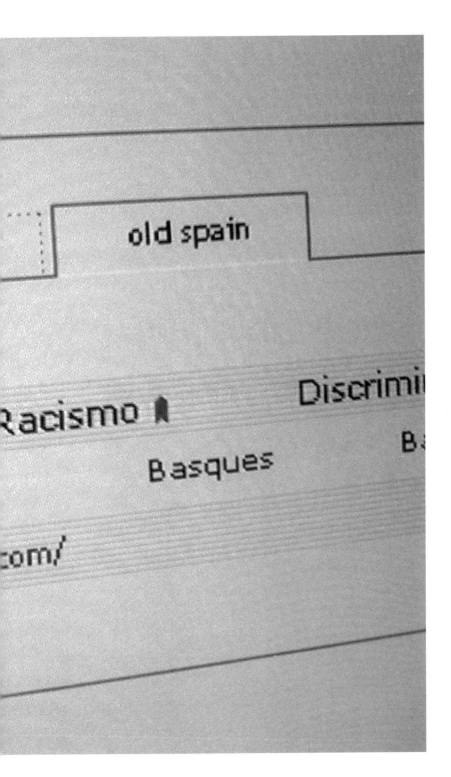

nuclear arms, and added to that demographic is then a religious element (pax christi). In a certain sense these ideal groups are stranger networks but they are not strange, because it is an ideal demographic. In a network the question is do you have an unfamiliarity. What's the unfamiliarity of the demographic? When the level is high you can speak of a stranger network.

Is the creation of a stranger network an indication of the urgency of a issue?

The process by which some form of collectivity produces some kind of urgency or what you can call issuefication, the issuefying of an issue, involves more than just refreshing pages. Traditionally, one could measure the level of urgency by the growth of the network and the frequency of issue statements, and by some sort of refreshing behaviour, the adding of content, and levels of info sharing. That's ideal typical. A high degree of strangeness and a high degree of network growth and intensity of issue statements, that is then urgency. Or heavy issuefication. You could have all those factors present and yet it still doesn't become 'urgent' or 'hot', that is, in the news.

Govcom.org, it seems, supplies its research with visual, cartographic evidence. Or is it the other way round, the maps providing the insight?

The practice is that it strives to build upon the notion of a social map. In some sense the visualization practice is based on this notion, but it strives to show another kind of reality than those that are constructed when traditionally one initiates a broader social discussion. In identifying who the stakeholders to a certain issue are, traditionally speaking you would have implicit assumptions about who is important. Whereas we ask the web to tell us who is important. So this is the new social map. In thinking about our cartographical work, then, you have to understand it as a 'notional' practice.

What is the spatial notion behind your cartographical work? What is actually depicted?

The language that is used on the web is a language of space. And over the past eight years web notions of space have changed. In the early days you had the notions of hyperspace or outerspace which later then gave way, largely because of public sphere theory, to notions about 'sphere' or 'spheres': the 'blogosphere', the 'logosphere' and the 'websphere'. More recently there is what I call the revenge of geography: when you type 'www.google.com' into your browser, you are redirected to google.nl, you're taken back home! We can dismiss the idea of the web as a placeless space. You're taken back home by default. We make visual contributions to these types of notions of space, most recently with the *Issue Geographer*. With your *Issue Crawler* results you can create an *Issue Crawler* network and plot this onto a geographical map. Why would you want to do that? Well, what we are doing is developing a critique of issue mobility or issue drift [when organizations or networks of organizations drift away from issues. Ed.], of organizations (governmental of nongovernmental) that move from summit to summit, and from one large dam project to another large dam project, and seeing the extent to which these organizations remember what's actually happening on the ground. Looking at the extent of issue abandonment because of the mobility of organizations. So we wanted to look at the distance between where an issue comes from and where an issue is based. The base being the network and the form being the ground. And also to look at the distributed geography of an issue. In each of these visualization projects, we not only research questions but we contribute to them critically.

How is your work used in the end? What is your reservoir? Is it 'the honour of thinking', as Lyotard suggested in The Postmodern Condition?

What we are dipping into is more like wading into the info sea. It is the insight into the degree to which the web can still be a kind of collision space for alternative forms of realities. In some sense our visualization work is making this collision space into a reality. Our reservoir is that insight. From what was previously termed source competition to what is now termed collision space.

Should the work of Govcom.org be understood as an indication or an expression of the public domain that you are studying?

We use advanced webmetrics in order to derive indicators of the state of the web. And ultimately the infographics we produce must also be understood as issue narratives, stories about the state of an issue, and as expressions of those states. So, unfortunately, they are both indicative as well as expressive.

A good part of our work is to prevent ourselves from being pushed into a corner. Never be just scientists, never be just visualizers, nor just designers, just software developers. We talk about science in artistic circles, we talk about art in scientific circles, because we have the web-insight that the action is always going on elsewhere.

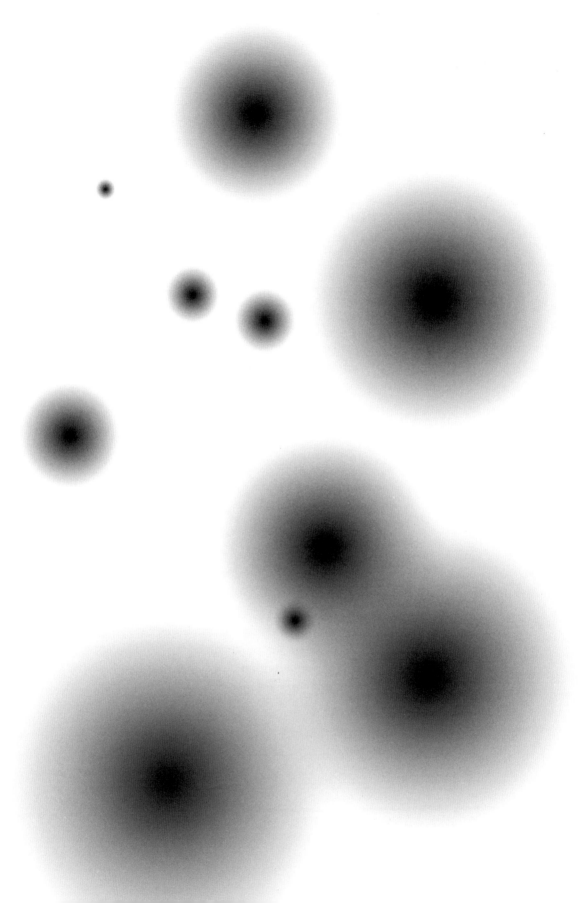

Hot Spot

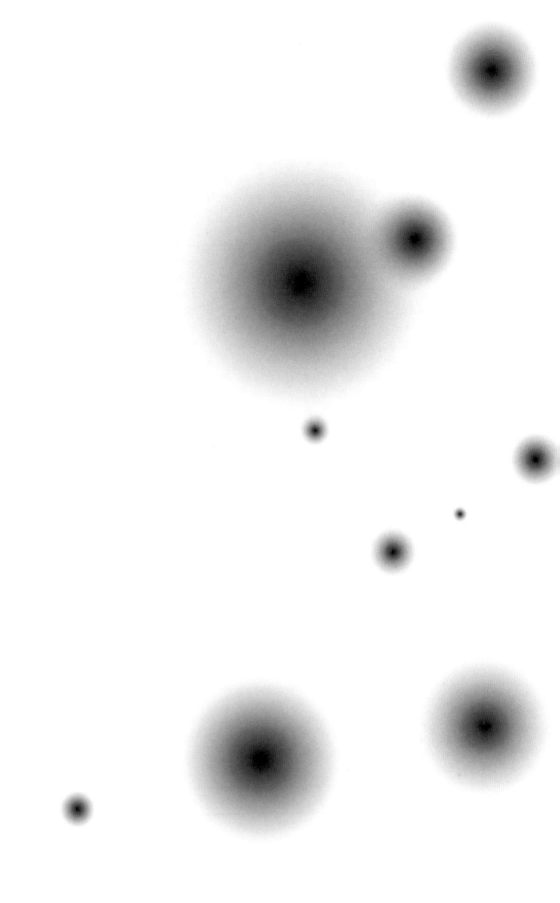

Geert van de Wetering

Hot Spot

Impetus Towards Innovation of Public Broadcasting

'Tell me something I don't know.' That was the subtitle of the proposal Bregtje van der Haak, programme maker at the VPRO, submitted to the Dutch Public Broadcasting Authority's Executive Board. Surprise me. Move me. And above all, inspire me with new ideas and passionate people. This brief forms the core of the initiative that since this January has borne the name Hot Spot and is set to run into 2008. After an intensive preparation process in which Bregtje van der Haak called in the assistance of Martijn de Waal and myself, the outlines of the project became discernible. Hot Spot is an informal, creative club for programme makers at all Dutch public broadcasters, which organizes regular gatherings at alternating locations. The aim is to come up with new ideas and to exchange thoughts, with an eye towards the future. Evenings are organized around a central theme, during which new technologies are discussed, social trends are examined and useful ideas are derived from such disciplines as fashion, design and the visual arts for application in public media. The evenings consist of presentations and discussions. Guests, well-known and unknown, speak about their own work and their ideas, often about a work in progress. Sneak previews, pilots and rushes are screened, but also websites and Power Point presentations.

The gatherings aim to provide an impetus to a 'public television culture', a television culture that is genuinely 'public', with a genuinely democratic significance and not based on ratings. Thinking about public broadcasting is too tied to money, power, structures and organization models. This is not conducive to the creativity of programme makers, who are the capital of the public broadcasting system. Creativity thrives in an open atmosphere, exchanges of thoughts and a continuous supply of new, inspiring ideas. For the future of public broadcasting, it is imperative to make room for innovations. And thus for a conversation about the profession. What do we want to make? Why? For whom?

These questions were the focus of the two Hot Spot evenings we organized prior to the summer of 2007. The first, entitled 'The Art Show', had as its premise the beauty of the original idea. Those in attendance were able to learn about innovative ideas and meet people who either come up with new ideas themselves or analyse and assess these ideas. Speakers included Gary Carter, chief creative officer with Fremantle Media, a large international media production company. He discussed the sense and the nonsense of searching for 'the next big thing'.

Tom Himpe, a London advertising executive, gave a presentation on 'guerilla advertising' – alternative, clandestine and original ways of hawking a product. This is significant not only for companies producing consumer goods, but also for programme makers, who in a constantly expanding media universe have to continually reposition themselves in order to attract the attention of the viewer or listener.

As part of the theme week 'Wij zijn de baas' ('We're the boss'), about the importance of democracy (October 2007), a second Hot Spot was organized around the question of how, as a public broadcaster, to generate a meaningful public debate using the latest technological advances. The essence of a democracy, after all, is that a free and public discussion is possible, one that actually contributes to the development of a society. To this end a number of guests were invited to develop ideas in collaboration with the programme makers on shaping this public debate. The guests included coordinators of popular weblogs on politics, artists, media philosophers, engineers and gaming developers.

During the Picnic cross-media week, a major Hot Spot event took place, concerning virtual worlds. A programme was put together in association with the Submarine production company on the opportunities that games and virtual worlds such as Second Life present to programme makers in addressing a new audience and in finding new forms for telling stories.

Future Hot Spot gatherings will focus on themes such as civic journalism, new narrative forms and ethnic diversity.

In addition to organizing these evenings, Hot Spot aims to establish short- or long-term alliances with various partners. These might be cultural institutions, platforms for new media, festivals, like Picnic, Nieuw Akademia, Submarine, all of which concentrate on organizing cross-media projects, but it might also be a magazine, for example. Indeed, this issue of *Open* is one such example.

Open No. 13 focuses on the question of how the 'public programme' is changing as a result of the effects of globalization and the digital age. This supplement zeroes in on the question of how public media are responding to new, more informal and individually oriented communication technologies, mobile media, media formats and media strategies. It attempts to bring these sometimes rather abstract developments back to the level of actual practice: what do these shifts signify for the programme maker? How should he or she relate to an audience that does not swallow everything docilely, how can he or she use the audience to positively influence his or her programme?

In his column, Dingeman Kuilman, director of the Premsela Foundation, a platform for Dutch design, compares two ways of using television: as a medium that records (the *camera obscura*) and as a medium that creates (the *lanterna magica*). In his view, television has become too much a medium that merely records the world around us. He wonders why current programmes are so lacking in creative content.

That programme makers must do better is without question. That they should be given more room to manoeuvre by courageous managers is equally clear. But will they then also get the critique they need? Many programme makers denounce the reviews of their broadcasts in daily and weekly newspapers. Not because these are purely negative, but because they often demonstrate so little insight into television and radio. Critics limit themselves primarily to what is said or done by whom in which programme. A solid analysis of how a programme is structured, how it is edited or how it is experienced is lacking.

This last point is discussed in the article by scientific researchers Irene Costera Meijer (media studies) and Maarten Reesink (television sciences), both at the University of Amsterdam. Their content analysis shows that television critics are very one-sided in their approach: they pay little attention to the commercial broadcasters and disproportionate attention to journalistic and cultural programmes. Most articles consist of strictly personal opinions that virtually relate solely to the content of the programming on offer. There is little or no attention for the aesthetics or the impact of television programmes. According to Costera Meijer and Reesink, critics should therefore develop an experience-oriented vocabulary in order to assess programmes differently.

But of course it all starts with the maker. It is he or she who needs to undergo a change in mentality. Whereas traditional programme makers mainly want to inform their audience, 'new' makers primarily want to communicate with their audience. Media philosopher Bas Könning cannot emphasize this new role often enough. In the interview in this issue he says, 'People today are far less satisfied with the status quo. And that is the result of the huge expansion of the supply and the flows of information. The user/viewer/listener is no longer dependent on you – it's the other way round. Far worse than that, the world can discuss you without you. That is something many programme makers are having trouble getting used to.' If you have a new idea for a programme, start your own blog immediately. That is Könning's imperative advice. Provide access to the process of genesis and you create not only your future audience, but there is a significant likelihood that you will explore new paths as a result of suggestions from the readers of your blog. So it's a two-way street.

That was in fact the experience of the radio play writer Bert Kommerij. He was, as he puts it, 'booted onto the internet' by the broadcaster for which he works. The RVU commissioned him to conduct research into the question of how people take control of their lives. And how they keep it.

And what role the internet plays in this. For this supplement, he submitted the visual contribution *Flick Radio – Makes my world feel real*. This contribution is based on the 'worklog' www.flickradio.nl. In it he is steadily reducing the difference between script and blog. He turns himself into a character and gives his new digital friends a voice. The end result will be a radio play (music and sound design by Marco Raaphorst) and an accompanying internet film, made with Flickr-photos complete with captions (editing by Pepijn Kortbeek).

Through the contributions in this supplement, we hope to provide a clearer picture of the shifts in media production, distribution and consumption. Although the processes upon which these shifts are based are often complex in nature, this does not mean that the efforts you have to make as a programme maker are enormous. The key is primarily a change in attitude toward the audience. The audience is no longer an anonymous receptor – the audience talks back and thinks along. The public itself is a producer as well. As a programmer, you can turn this to your advantage.

Dingeman Kuilman

Column

A Plea for the Magic Lantern

The fact that public broadcasting is regarded as belonging to the creative industry cannot conceal the sad state of creativity in this sector. Radio, television and internet display a striking lack of imaginative power, a situation that becomes even more embarrassing when set against the vigour of other creative sectors.

Why, for example, is no one in Hilversum[1] making programmes with a cachet to match that of our architecture and our design?

1. Hilversum, a city some 30 km southeast of Amsterdam, is the centre of Dutch broadcasting.

Stefan Themerson, writer, filmmaker, publisher and poet, distinguishes two ways of making images: the camera obscura and the magic lantern. The camera obscura represents reality. The magic lantern by contrast elevates representation to the status of reality. Each of these principles results in a different approach to public broadcasting as a creative medium: do programme makers accept existing reality for what it is? Or do they manipulate reality by allowing their imagination free play?

Jaap Drupsteen (b. 1942) belongs to the second category. Drupsteen trained as a graphic designer.

In 1975, following a sensational series of vpro network promo spots, he produced his first major feature: *Het grote gebeuren* (The Great Happening). The action, based on a short story by Belcampo, takes place on the Day of Judgement in the Overijssel village of Rijssen. Hordes of devils and angels descend on the village to read the inhabitants their final lesson. After all the villagers have been carried off to heaven or to hell, only Belcampo, disguised as a devil, remains behind. Eventually, after

a group of angels discovers him, he is conveyed heavenwards, 'with steady wingbeats'.

I still recall the New Year's Eve when *Het grote begeuren* was broadcast. The sense of witnessing something completely new was overwhelming.

Jaap Drupsteen says of this work: 'The viewer is repeatedly fucked about', thereby revealing himself to be no devotee of today's phone-in quizzes. Rather, he champions the programme maker as illusionist. He takes issue with television's alleged social benefit: 'Everything that's added is nonsense, personal hobbies, artistic claptrap, fake magic, pomposity, technical tours de force, trendy hype and showing off, which usually

undermines the functionality and for that reason is infinitely more interesting.'

No one looking at the way things have developed since the 1980s can avoid the conclusion that Jaap Drupsteen's views are out of date. Television, radio and internet have become reality machines: the 'Big Brother' living room and the 'Golden Cage' villa turn television quite literally into a camera obscura.

So where did things go wrong with the magic lantern? This was a question Jaap Drupsteen asked himself in 1985, when the NOS[2] refused to enter his music theatre production *The Flood* in the Prix Italia. He vented his frustration in several interviews: 'If the NOS enters something it's more likely to be a recording of a good performance. But that's more to the credit of the theatre makers than the TV makers. . . . That's typical of the views on creativity and innovation. It's completely normal for television to appropriate the creativity of other media. . . . I've always found that a bit parasitical. But when a production in which television itself is used as creative medium is brushed aside as an incident, I'm rather dismayed.'

Drupsteen regards television as a creative medium, especially

2. NOS is the Dutch acronym for the state-funded Netherlands Broadcasting Foundation.

public television and the public broadcasting system as a whole. Public broadcasting is public space. Public space is free space. Free space is a space for imagination. Or should be, at any rate.

The international success of Dutch architecture and design is due not just to training, talent and a little money, but above all to good clients. Not to managers, who hide behind public approval and taste, but to people of character with the courage to take responsibility for complete and partial failures. Open-minded and open-hearted. Convinced of the need to stimulate public curiosity.

If public broadcasters are serious about rediscovering their creativity, they must start by being good clients. Who will give the old and new Drupsteens the opportunity to conquer public space? As long as no one feels the need to do so, even the illusionists can have no illusions.

Geert van de Wetering

'The Focus Is on the Process'

Interview with Bas Könning

BK In the 1980s I studied visual communications at the AKI Academy of Visual Arts in Enschede. After that I went on to study philosophy in Amsterdam, for the most part as a ghost student, because I'd used up my university time. I mainly took courses in linguistic philosophy. Around that time I also became fascinated by the internet, which at that moment was nothing more than a collection of bulletin boards. Yet its users could already sense that it was going to turn into something amazing.

From 1994 onward I advised businesses and government and educational institutions on integrating the internet into their organizations. I handled the entire process, like a one-man band, from designing the websites and data structures to initiating the staff into its mysteries. Now that the other media have also become part of the digital revolution, these are really great times for a media philosopher. Incidentally, don't confuse a media philosopher with a media analyst. Aside from analysis, a philosopher lavishes most of his care on synthesis. I examine how developments in the media are changing the world and vice versa. A new media landscape is emerging, and I am sketching a picture of it. My day-to-day work consists of surfing the web a lot, and I work on various projects in conjunction with Nieuw Akademia, a network of academics, consultants and artists. At the moment I am involved, via Nieuw Akademia, with the NPOX* media festival organized by the Dutch public broadcasters.

*On 19 and 20 November 2007, the NPOX Media Festival, intended for public broadcasters, will be held at the Institute for Sound and Vision in Hilversum. Current developments In the media are leading to numerous forms of fragmentation: fragmentation of media platforms, fragmentation of reach and fragmentation of society into subcultures. The answer to this is to create cross-overs: cross-media, cross-community, cross-culture. This has been the domain of public broadcasting from its very beginning – in fact public broadcasting is the precursor of the creation of cross-overs and the cultivation of new possibilities. This is not always recognized, however, whether inside or outside the broadcasting system. The NPOX media festival aims to change this, by showing what is already being done, to examine what the next steps might be and thereby provide a stimulus to further development of innovative products among public broadcasting organizations.

What is the difference between the current excitement about the web and the internet hype of the late 1990s?

Back then we could see the potential, but it was not yet clear what the value of these possibilities was. One could see, for instance, that the supply of products and information was growing enormously. It was assumed that the audience would appreciate this a lot, because freedom of choice seemed a major positive at the time. Since then, it has been demonstrated more and more frequently that what we want is not a broad selection, that we in fact want things to be pre-selected for us. These days you can see that a lot more hierarchy is emerging than in the late 1990s, even though the amount on offer is several orders of magnitude greater, and so is the chaos. The present hierarchy is user-driven, that is to say the sender has made it possible for the receptors to apply a hierarchy to the content on offer, through 'tagging' (describing and labelling), 'rating' (validating) and 'sharing'. We encounter 'familiar strangers' – strangers, but with the same preferences. In this way, the web is evolving from a search engine into a finding machine, and that is an essential transformation, because most people don't enjoy searching very much.

The use of media has changed enormously. What is the most significant shift?

The most significant development, in my view, is the blurring of the boundaries between the various information and communication platforms. Familiar media such a television, radio, internet, newspapers and telephones are making way for a broad palette of hybrid forms. There are more and more devices that can more or less do everything. Like a telephone on which you can watch video. The display screen will soon compete with the printed newspaper at the breakfast table. And slowly but surely, the possibilities of the internet are being made available on television. These are initially technological developments, but they are altering behaviour, as well as the expectations of the audience toward all media. For years, participating in television was not an option. We took that for granted, but the younger generations no longer do. Of the 100 per cent that consume video via internet, 10 per cent respond or participate. That does not seem like much, but the 90 per cent that do not respond themselves do find it very important that the possibility exists. Among these responses, after all, are familiar strangers, who represent their voice. And 1 per cent of internet users put their own material on the web. So at least 1 in 100 consumers becomes a producer if given the chance. This changes the perception of the media and therefore the role of the programme maker – he or she is now among equals, the audience is media-savvy and the programme maker will have to behave accordingly.

Is a change in mentality required for the majority of programme makers?

My short answer would be no, they should just go on making beautiful things. But it is a fact that beautiful things are not automatically seen by their intended audience. So it helps if programme makers become aware of new ways of reaching the audience, and better still, involve the audience in the production process.

What we do or do not watch is increasingly channelled through our own networks and communities. In these communities there are always key figures: people who are more present than the rest, who pop up all over the place and link the flows of information. Programme makers are well-advised to seek out these 'connectors'. They are worth their weight in gold to programme makers, for they know what's going on. And they also take care of distribution, for once connectors find out about something, it quickly gets around.

What is the difference in approach between a traditional programme maker and a programme maker who is abreast of all the new developments in the realm of media production, distribution and use?

The traditional maker handles the research phase from within his or her own network. His or her focus is a medium: it will be a television or radio programme in a specific time slot. The broadcast is mostly the first and often also the last contact for the audience. After the broadcast he or she uses his or her network to see whether something extra can be done with the programme: a discussion evening in the De Balie cultural centre, hiring it out to institutions or a presentation at a university. In short, he or she uses the structure, the platforms and the institutions he or she knows.

For a 'new' maker the time slot is an important climax as well, but the focus is on the process. He or she gets involved in networks related to the subject, sees this as the first audience to be won over and potentially turned into a source. He or she starts a blog, and responds to other blogs. He or she creates circles around his or her production process, adds familiar strangers to his or her address book, turns them into accomplices, puts raw material on YouTube and Hyves, provokes reactions.

Among traditional media makers you sometimes detect fear or at least scepticism in relation to processes of collective and collaborative intelligence. Fear of compromising the quality of the news gathering and the reliability of information. Is this fear justified?

Not at all. The debate that has always raged within journalism – about the vetting of information and about objectivity and subjectivity – is now often being waged by the audience. A much more intricate web of gradual truth has emerged. Every web user, children definitely included, knows that doubt is permissible and imperative. Something is provisionally true, or plausible, or good enough to pass on, with or without source attribution.

The surfeit of examples in which nuanced gradations of the truth exist has made the audience increasingly more adept at assessing the news as to truth value. What used to be done solely by the journalist is now done by the receptor: collecting sources, weighing and testing. If possible he or she does this in consultation with other users, for without supplemental communication, information is less interesting anyway, whether it is true or not.

Geert Lovink, in his article elsewhere in this issue, is sceptical about the expected overthrow of the traditional mass media. He sees precious little evidence of it. What is your prediction?

The mass media have already sustained a major blow, particularly as a result of the expansion of supply, and are increasingly targeting specific groups or themes. In the 1970s, the Dutch television evening news reached 55 per cent of the public; now all the Dutch television channels put together can barely achieve that. Yet despite this growing fragmentation, mass media will retain a certain position. First, because we want stars, and stars exist and thrive by the grace of the mass media. A hit on YouTube only genuinely becomes a hype once the mass media start reporting on it. And I don't see this changing any time soon.

In addition, chatting about yesterday's media in schoolyards and office canteens is a widely shared pleasure, and therefore a programme watched by a lot of people will continue to exert a gravitational effect. Mass media are also indispensable for the creation of frames of reference. Without a regular experience of common ground, it is difficult to be one society. For this reason, governments will work hard to preserve the mass media. The commercial channels, however, are in for a tough time. Advertisers, en masse, are looking for new ways to reach the consumer, and the boom in store for on-demand television is a threat to commercial breaks. It is not yet clear what will happen, but that *something* is going to change is certain.

Which book or which blog is really of quintessential importance if you, as a programme maker/media maker, want to be thoroughly abreast of the latest developments in the media ecosystem?

Your own blog! With any luck you'll be automatically kept on your toes by your readers. And then you don't have to read all of those books about developments in the use of media. I haven't read Chris Anderson's bestseller, *The Long Tail*, but I know exactly what's in it. I followed various discussions of *The Long Tail* on the web and am now familiar not only with Anderson's insights, but also with those of his critics. And the critique of that critique. That is the blessing of participation in the media.

Irene Costera Meijer & Maarten Reesink

Television, Criticism and the Wow Factor

Sometime in the late 1990s, Maarten Reesink took part in a forum on various forms of reality and 'emotion' television, organized by the University of Maastricht. The two other forum participants were Frits Abrahams, then the NRC *Handelsblad* newspaper's regular television critic, and Pieter Storms, maker of the notorious consumer advocacy programme *Breekijzer*, who took offence that a scientist would label his programme 'emotion television'. No offence was intended, Reesink argued, for 'emotion television' can in fact have all sorts of positive qualities – something Abrahams, on the other hand, felt to be nonsense: one should not justify something that is bad, certainly not as an academic. You will have guessed that the discussion lasted late into the night, too late to head home all the way across the country, which is why the organization had reserved rooms for all the forum participants in the adjacent three-star hotel.

The next morning, Abrahams, rightfully considered by many to be the best television critic in the Netherlands, announced that now that he had slept on it, there was something, after all, in science's more nuanced view of the new genre. And in fact, in the time he had been a television critic, he had never opened an academic book about television. Nor was he about to do so: his career as a television critic had nearly run its course, and, far more significantly, he was no longer able to absorb such a completely different view of the medium of television. That other vocabulary, those new perspectives, all those nuances and aspects would have to be left to a new generation of critics to take up.

TV Know-How?

This, however, has not come to pass. In 2001 Marieke van Leeuwen graduated with a thesis entitled *Kwaliteit ontketend: argumenten voor een nieuwe televisiekritiek* (Quality Unleashed: Arguments for a New Television Criticism). It is the report of a content analysis of all television reviews in a selection of national and regional daily newspapers in the Netherlands over a period of one year. The results are revealing: for 12 months, there was not a single positive review of a programme broadcast on a Dutch commercial channel in any of these newspapers. There was scarcely any attention at all paid to the commercial channels: the television critics displayed a disproportionate amount of attention to news and culture programmes by the public broadcasters. The majority of the reviews consisted of strictly personal opinions and focused, virtually exclusively, on the content of the programme offerings. Little attention, if any, was paid to the aesthetics or the impact of the television programmes.

As a rule, literature, classical music and even films are discussed by people who are well-versed in these disciplines. But anyone familiar to any extent with the views of the French cultural sociologist Pierre Bourdieu understands what constitutes the basis of television criticism: the articles are a fairly representative reflection of the sociocultural preferences of a specific professional class, which is considerably coherent along a number of lines (for instance education, ethnicity, gender). Add a pinch of elitism if necessary and a few grains of social desirability, and an explanation for the unearthed results begins to fall into place. (Bourdieu, incidentally, did not display much understanding of television in his essay *On Television*.)[1] In order to give their columns – for that is what these reviews essentially were – some added value, Dutch television critics have opted en masse for the humorous approach. With a few rare exceptions, our professional couch potatoes are without a doubt the funniest guys in the room. Puns and other witticisms, bizarre comparisons and the most creative of segues, nothing is too crazy for the Dutch scribblers. There is one downside: these extremely pleasurable, highly readable pieces too often demonstrate even more superficiality than the programmes they condemn.

1. Pierre Bourdieu, *Sur la télévision* (Paris: Raisons d'agir, 1996) transl. as *On Television* (New York: The New Press, 1998).

What Is Quality Television?

Yet a change seems to be gradually taking place in the nature and tone of television reviews. Commercial and popular programmes are being increasingly taken seriously. In April 2007, at the presentation of the Lira Award for best television drama, jury member and television critic for the weekly *De Groene Amsterdammer* Walter van der Kooi even said that some commercial drama productions were 'absolutely worth watching. Net 5's *Evelien*, in particular, based on the character created by Martin Bril (directed by Rita Horst, written by Karin van der Meer) proved to be a welcome newcomer.'[2] Conversely, some critics are occasionally expressing criticism about the uninspiring quality of serious programmes such as the news and discussion programmes *Buitenhof* or *Nova*. In the newspaper *de Volkskrant*, Wim de Jong even attempted to describe his positive feelings at watching a new KRO reality series, *Gezellig naar de Krim* (Happy campers on the road to the Crimea, more or less).[3]

2. Walter van der Kooi, 'Het niveau. De LIRA-nominaties van 2007', *De Groene Amsterdammer*, 9 May 2007.

3. Wim de Jong, 'Sleurhut', *de Volkskrant*, 20 June 2007.

A good illustration of the limits of the profession's vocabulary of quality is that he did not get much beyond indicating what the programme is *not*. It is not an 'emo-format'. No one gets killed. No one has to get voted off because money has to be made off text messages from the call-in audience. No farmers or other desperate singles are matched up, no long-lost lovers are reunited. And there was not even any participant 'who had to address the camera in isolation in order to share his or her private feelings about the group process with the viewers at home.'

Reviewers apparently still find it difficult to identify the qualities of new genres such as reality soaps. In that they are not alone. Television makers have not figured this out either. How are we supposed to label the aesthetic qualities of *De Gouden Kooi* (a *Big Brother*-like show with millionaire participants), or explain why hundreds of thousands of people watch with bated breath as pop singer Frans Bauer puts up a picture in his house on his reality show? The explanation for this is that we actually do not really know how to judge quality on television: there is no vocabulary with which to discuss it, and there is not even the beginning of a framework within which you would be able to. To judge news and background pieces, therefore, we resort to values and standards developed within journalism; for drama we can appeal to all manner of quality criteria from the world of the cinema and the theatre. But when genres begin to cross over (which is increasingly the case in television), or worse, when television starts to develop genres of its own that do not have origins in other media or disciplines, we are at a loss for words: how in heaven's name can we then still recognize, let alone judge, quality on television?

Is Quality Good?

As a rule, quality is considered a positive term; it is a recommendation to watch or listen to something. For the VPRO broadcasting organization, Irene Costera Meijer, with several researchers and a large number of students, looked into the meaning of 'quality' for the audience.[4] We concentrated our survey on the group that is the VPRO's quintessential target audience, higher-educated, vocal citizens, a.k.a. the 'quality audience'. Our respondents included television reviewers and columnists. For this group, quality was automatically linked to certain informational genres.

4. Irene Costera Meijer, et al., 'De ervaring van kwaliteit'. Part of the research report *De Magie van Kwaliteit* (Hilversum: VPRO/UVA, March 2007).

'Ordinary' viewers were not so sure about the word 'quality'. They too connected quality with serious informational programmes, but also with 'boring' and 'slow'. The fact that a programme was known as a 'quality programme' did not always prove to be a recommendation. 'Quality' was seen by a large proportion of the audience more as a genre characteristic of serious drama and serious information than as a neutral evaluation dimension that would induce them to watch. The viewer associates quality with good and important programmes, but not necessarily with interesting or appealing ones.

Quality as Experience

In the conventional understanding of quality, the quality of a programme is measured by intrinsic or content-based aspects of programmes. In this context, a news programme is considered to be of quality, for instance, when it fulfils the essential criteria of quality journalism.

> Tessa (36, administrative assistant): Zomergasten (an interview programme), Thema-avonden (evenings of themed programming on the public channels), Tegenlicht (a documentary series) and Buitenhof (a news discussion programme) are programmes that go in depth, provide greater insight into people, society. And provide critique.

From this standpoint, media users want television, radio and internet to keep them 'up to date' and 'inform' them about what is going on in the world. Without good information, after all, one cannot be a good citizen.

> Wessel (65, television critic): Look, I cannot do without the NOS Journaal (the public broadcaster's nightly news programme), even though I am very critical of it, but what can you do. . . The same is true of Buitenhof. I find Buitenhof an unbelievably boring programme, but important things are said in it.

The label of 'boring' for the *Buitenhof* programme illustrates how even television critics are gradually adopting new standards of quality for informational programmes. This is echoed by a VPRO programme maker: '*Tegenlicht* is good and respectable. But it's like with a man. Good and respectable is often boring as well.' While television viewers (continue to) deem *Tegenlicht* a quality programme, they would like to see it be 'more fun', 'lighter' and 'more entertaining'. This is not so much about the issues, incidentally, as about their presentation and treatment.

> Marieke (25, physical therapist): It [Tegenlicht] is rather dry, so I do think a little bit of entertain-

> ment wouldn't hurt. Not when it comes to the issues
> they cover, because that really is hyper-super . . .
> You shouldn't joke about that, but there are items,
> for instance, with which something fun could be done.
> Or just a light documentary made about it. Something
> that's just outlined and not gone over with a super-
> critical light.

Viewers have become more critical and are making greater demands of television. A programme, as Costera Meijer showed in an earlier survey, should not only be informative, or well-made – it should also be gripping.[5] A programme has quality if it manages to 'touch you', 'grab you', 'inspire' you, 'trigger' something, 'fan the flames a little', 'grab you by the throat', 'touch you emotionally', 'do something to you', 'arouse emotions', allow you to 'get caught up in it', be 'moved' by it. This is just a small sample of the words used by our respondents to make clear when they felt a pro-gramme was good.

5. Irene Costera Meijer, *De toekomst van het nieuws* (Amsterdam: Otto Cramwinckel, 2006).

> Wim (50, film maker): I don't have much use for yet
> another documentary explaining how the bio-industry
> works. At a certain point I've had enough . . . It
> doesn't shock me enough. What I would find more inter-
> esting is contrast. I love that. Show how our agricul-
> tural surplus is used to produce energy, to produce
> electricity. Contrast that with a story about the
> famine in the Sudan . . . That's when it gets really
> intense and you see how out of balance it all is.

These higher standards set by viewers coincide with a general trend scientists identify as the shift from an information society to an experience society. People are no longer looking for pure information from the media; instead they want newspapers, magazines and broadcasters to make them experience something that stimulates their imaginations. The normative criterion for quality shifts from 'informed citizenship' to the 'quality of life'.

Feel-Good Quality and Wow Quality

Henry Jenkins connects quality with the 'wow climax'.[6] If a programme has you sitting on the edge of your seat, this experience can stay with you for a long time.

6. Henry Jenkins, *The Wow Climax. Tracing the Emotional Impact of Popular Culture* (New York/London: New York University Press, 2007).

> Hans (44, photographer): That's the way it was in De wandelende tak (a radio programme on world music) and this was a very beautiful sound excerpt someone had taped in New Guinea, I think . . . Because someone had died and the song was about that. And you heard it slowly come up the path and then fade away. Now that was such beautiful, atmospheric radio. And yes, that touches me. It's been really ten years ago, uh, now maybe I'm exaggerating, but it was definitely six years ago or thereabouts. So it was that long ago and I can still remember it so well.

The respondents we interviewed distinguish two kinds of quality experiences in this context. We use the term 'wow experience' for the experience of being completely caught up in a programme (comparable with the experience of computer game players) and the 'feel-good experience' for the experience of simple relaxed enjoyment. We describe the 'wow experience' as a quality *effort*, comparable to Maslow's peak experience.[7] The 'feel-good experience' is about quality *relaxation*. Yet according to the audience, this quality too contributes something to their lives. Such a programme is easy to watch or listen to, it absorbs, does not irritate, because it is well made. It represents experiencing pleasure without requiring too much energy and attention.

7. Robert Kubey and Mihaly Csikszentmihalyi, *Television and the Quality of Life. How Viewing Shapes Everyday Experience* (Hillsdale: Lawrence Erlbaum Associates, Publishers, 1990).

> Lizette (25, project manager): I like De wereld draait door (a daily discussion programme) and watch it often . . . I find it a pleasant programme to watch after a busy workday. It's light, but it deals with real issues. Unlike RTL Boulevard (a daily gossip programme), for example, which is broadcast at the same time.

Relaxed enjoyment is not the same as simple diversion. Our respondents are quite honest about this: they too watch programmes or channels just to kill time on occasion. Programmes like *Big Brother* and *Jensen!* (a 'shock jock'-type talk show) and youth-oriented radio station *FunX* were cited in this context. Fun every once in a while when you don't feel like doing anything, but you don't stay home for it, you don't feel involved, you don't record it and seldom give it your full attention. For children, cartoons often fulfil this function of 'killing time'.

If the existing content-focused vocabulary of quality were to be expanded by means of an experience-focused vocabulary, television critics might have more tools with which to provide us, as viewers, insights into the significance of programmes. Whether a programme has quality can then no longer be determined solely from its content. Quality is also demonstrated by the experience of the programme. Does it contribute something to the quality of life? A really good programme does not have to lead to questions in parliament, but it should add something of value to the communication within the community for which it is intended. It facilitates and supports self-determination. The relationship of the programme maker with his or her subject can also be judged in more dimensions. The use of words like 'critical' and 'independent' indicates a content-focused idiom of quality; 'grounded', 'involved', 'inspiring', 'personal' and 'self-reflecting' indicate an impact-focused idiom of quality. In the former, when the approach to a subject is discussed, dimensions of classical journalism such as 'objective', 'neutral', 'rational' and 'nuanced' automatically come up. They do not even have to be cited. When the approach is aimed, on the other hand, at the viewer's 'passion' and 'compassion', and demonstrates colour instead of shades of grey, the programme maker is quickly judged to have let him or herself get carried away by his or her subject, or have failed to maintain sufficient distance. Perhaps reviewers (but also programme makers) might alternate their critical tone once in a while with inspiring, unique and enthusiasm-rousing stories about programmes? We expect a broader vocabulary of quality to improve the quality of television criticism.

Bert Kommerij

Flick Radio

'Makes the World Feel Real for Me'

A Dutch man meets an unusual,
American teenager on the internet.
They describe their lives by means of
various photos.
Distances are great, contact becomes
more and more intimate.
Until the writer invites her to become
the main character in a story he is
planning to write.
The girl withdraws, the man is left
behind with the photos.

1.

It gradually dawns on me.
On Flickr you don't collect photos, but people.
It is particularly close and efficient in the Addict group.
That's how I got in touch yesterday with Kendra, an 18-year old schoolgirl from Minnesota.
I saw she'd written a paper on her Flickr addiction.
So I asked to see it.
Now we're contacts.

BERT
Do you think YouTube addicts are different than Flickr addicts?
KENDRA
I guess so, but I'm not sure.
Flickr makes the world feel real for me.

2.

Today she's not feeling well.

Shitty, in fact.

She's stayed home and is worrying about her
future.

Whether to finish school or not.

She has problems with her father and has an
unhappy love life.

No-one understands her.

Meanwhile her ambitions are piling up.

For Kendra the internet is reality.

A place to complain and to have fun, too.

She's not ashamed of anything.

3.

KENDRA

Wow Bert, this is beautiful!

BERT

Thank you, Kendra.

It's what I see when I look to the right.

(Computer is on the left.)

KENDRA

Very nice. I could sit and view that all day.

BERT

Yes, I know. But the computer doesn't accept
that.

Needs attention too.

KENDRA

Yes! Hahaha.

I want to go to Amsterdam so bad.

Bert

Really?

What do you expect of Amsterdam?

I mean . . . We're talking about . . . Holland.

KENDRA

I've been there. I just want to go there again.

BERT

Are there any specific places that I need to visit
for you?

KENDRA

What do you mean?

BERT

I could go there, make a photograph of it and
put it on Flickr.

(Then I will be forced to leave my view.

That's good.

I work at home most of the time, you see.

Almost never go outside.)

KENDRA

That isn't stupid at all!!

Hmm.

I don't know, it has been a good four years
since I was there, but, go outside and
photograph your favourite building?

I can't make you but that'd be neat.

I'd do the same here but it is winter.

BERT

True.

Freezing here too, with snow to come!

I never look at buildings as favourite or non-
favourite.

Favourite buildings are buildings with
remarkable stories, I guess . . .

There are some.

KENDRA

So awesome having a new, soon to be good
friend in another country! Grin! Huggles!

BERT

I think so too, Kendra.

I was in New York twice.

My friend Piet lived there for a year.

When I think of America I see lots of nature
and skyscrapers.

PS: I'm not into hugging.

Typical Dutch.

Grins are always welcome.

KENDRA

Too funny . . . the whole time I was writing
that comment I was like REMEMBER HE'S
DUTCH, THEY DON'T LIKE HUGS.

Oh well! Now I know.

Nature and skyscrapers is America land for
sure.

BERT

What a great conversation we have, if I may
say so.

The first time I saw her face, I got a shock.
A discontented, angry expression, looking
straight at the camera. Black-framed
spectacles.
Ugly hair.
The texts she'd posted were direct and honest.

She hates school, is moody and can't wait to
grow up.
She wants to be an artist.
She's chosen a course in medical photography,
but first she has to graduate from high school.
A sensible foundation.
Her portraits are pure, in my opinion. Time
and again.
She's not especially pretty, but average.
She's not afraid to portray herself as ugly, and
attends hard-rock concerts.
When she feels bad, she puts the camera right
in front of her face.
At times when others would avoid the mirror,
she zooms in.
She's not embarrassed about anything.
I'm especially envious of that.
She hides nothing, because she has nothing to
hide.
The public domain is where she feels at home.
She says: I'm not alone. Look at me.
Since I met Kendra everything's a lot nicer.

KENDRA

Hi Bert

BERT

Hi Kendra

KENDRA

I went to school this morning, took my Math
test and left.

Now I'm home again and going to bed.

I feel like shit.

I should quit school.

Leave them alone.

I took this picture with all my messy hair.

It's nothing.

4.

Kendra was different from everybody else.
You noticed her.

BERT
Hello Kendra.
This is Amsterdam calling.
Coming to cheer you up.
We only met yesterday, but still I can see you
are a very creative person.
This is a blessing and hell at the same time.
Strangely enough you feel terrible now,
but your pictures are getting better!
Also the texts.
Please never give up writing and taking
pictures when you feel like shit.
Think of all the people who are not able to
write and take pictures when they feel down.
I dare to say that you are a lucky person,
although I know it's not easy.
PS: Just go and get your diploma.
It's nothing.

What makes you love Flickr so much?
What is it that made you use Flickr in the first
place?
Flickr is my home.
I can't change my ways.
I feel like I belong here.
I am someone here.
Someone people respect and love me for who
I am.
Flickr makes my day, every day.

6.

'As younger people reveal their private lives
on the internet, the older generation looks
on with alarm and misapprehension not seen
since the early days of rock and roll.
The future belongs to the uninhibited.

'Change 1: They think of themselves as having
an audience
Change 2: They have archived their
adolescence
Change 3: Their skin is thicker then yours.'
(Emily Nussbaum, 'Say Everything', *New York
Magazine*, 12 February 2007.)

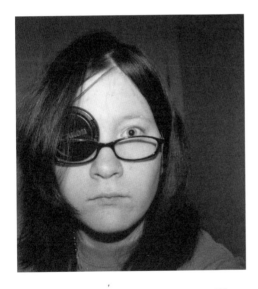

5.

KENDRA
I always have these weird visions
about what I want to do on Flickr,
how I want to make my daily picture,
where I wanna go and take pictures.
I live, breath, think, Flickr.
I feel like as if it is drug sometimes.
Could you live without Flickr?

7.

BERT
Kendra,
is it alright if I copy your Flickr-eyed
picture and text and put it on my work-log
www.flickradio.nl?
To show Dutch people how great Flickr is?
For me you are the ultimate Miss Flickr.
And I'm happy to be your audience.

KENDRA
Of course, Bert I gotta spread the love some
way, some how, and if I got a friend that'll help
spread the love, I must let him!
Go for it, dude.

9.

People's reactions vary.
Some are against the public character.
You've got guts, they say, you think you're
important.
They don't want to be in the photos and they
don't want me to write about them.
They've got strange ideas about the audience.
They don't know Kendra.

8.

I take the camera with me in the evening too,
when I'm walking Jules.
My walk through the neighbourhood is
different from what it used to be.
I see more. Of that I'm sure.
Also, I love Jules more since I've been putting
her photos on line. I don't exactly understand
how that's possible, but it's certainly true.

10.

BERT
Kendra, I would like to write about you.
Would you like to be the main character in my
story, my script?

KENDRA
Bert, I take that as a compliment so don't
mind at all!!!

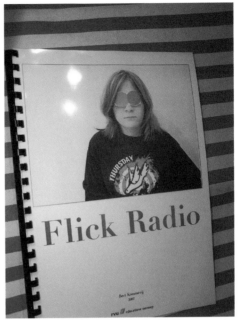

11.

When I was 17 I took my first photo.
A field full of dandelions.
In the same way that Kendra takes photos of
herself, I took them of dandelions.
I never thought about taking photos of myself.
There was nothing to see.
I wore big spectacles and my curls hung down
to my chin.
An 'I'm not there' adolescent.
At mealtimes I stuck my fingers in my ears,
because I couldn't stand eating noises.

When you look at a photo, you never think of
the photographer.
What he looked like.
How old he was.
Whether it was a man or a woman who
pressed the button.
(You're there and you're not there: you exist in
the other person.)
Kendra photographs what I would have liked
to have photographed.

12.

KENDRA
Hey that's me. :D
BERT
Yes, you are my main character.
KENDRA
Cute idea, darling. :] I figured.
BERT
I will do some translations and send it to you.
KENDRA
Sweet, I'm very grateful I can inspire you, like
you inspire me!
My electronic mail address is in my user info. I
really miss writing.
BERT
Title of the script is Flick Radio.
Both of us will be played by actors I guess.
The program will be online as mp3, so you can
listen to it as well on your computer.
We all play ourselves.
KENDRA
All right, that's nifty! :]
BERT
Nifty indeed.

13.

Kendra is pissed off with Flickr because she's realized that her entire social life's a mess.
She spends more time on Flickr than in the pub, the street or with friends.
She gets plenty of support from fellow addicts for her confession.
Her network grows and grows.
I wrote her that she's probably got mild burn-out.
And that the internet gives and takes.
You have to find the right balance somewhere along the edge.
Pseudo becomes real and real becomes digi and everything gets upside down.

KENDRA
I wish I had money
so I can travel.

Even if money doesn't make me happy
My goal is to be amazing
MAN
But you already are
Serious
KENDRA
I am bored . . .
My photos suck lately . . .
MAN
No
KENDRA
Yes
MAN
They are good
KENDRA
I try to be good
MAN
You are good
You dont have to try
KENDRA
I don't

14.

As soon as you are on the internet you look in the mirror.
It immediately shows you what you're doing.
You look for yourself in every task.
It's both therapeutic and confrontational.
It records processes, makes them visible.
Every click of the mouse defines you, and what you do, what affects, stimulates or drives you.
Your favourites form a fingerprint of your

hobbies, your interests.

Show me your favourites and I know who you are, or would like to be.

Your identity grows, is makeable, expands every day.

You become an archive, you pile up.

Work and private life blend together seamlessly.

It's a matter of organization.

Speed gives you a feeling of control, of power.

I form the internet as it forms me.

16.

It's getting real, Kendra. We will all become fiction.

15.

Kendra's Flickr addiction was getting out of control.

She painted make-up round her eyes, a patch of red and a patch of blue: the colours of the Flickr logo.

She keeps her eyes closed, though she could easily have had them open.

Yesterday in the city I saw two parasols on a balcony: one red, one blue.

I thought of Kendra and took a photo.

Now it's her favourite photo.

Addicts everywhere.

Plus a short chat.

Photos: Kendra Chaparral (CC License. Some rights reserved) and Bert Kommerij.

www.flickradio.nl is a RVU drama production 2007 and will be made with the support of the Netherlands Foundation for Cultural Broadcasting Productions.
Idea, script and direction: Bert Kommerij.
Sound design (under Creative Commons License): Marco Raaphorst. Visualization: Pepijn Kortbeek.
With thanks to Roswitha Kamps, Piet Marsman and Jaap Vermeer.
Final editing: Monique Mourits.

The texts in this article are from Kommerij's worklog www.flickr.nl and have been incorporated in the script of Flick Radio.

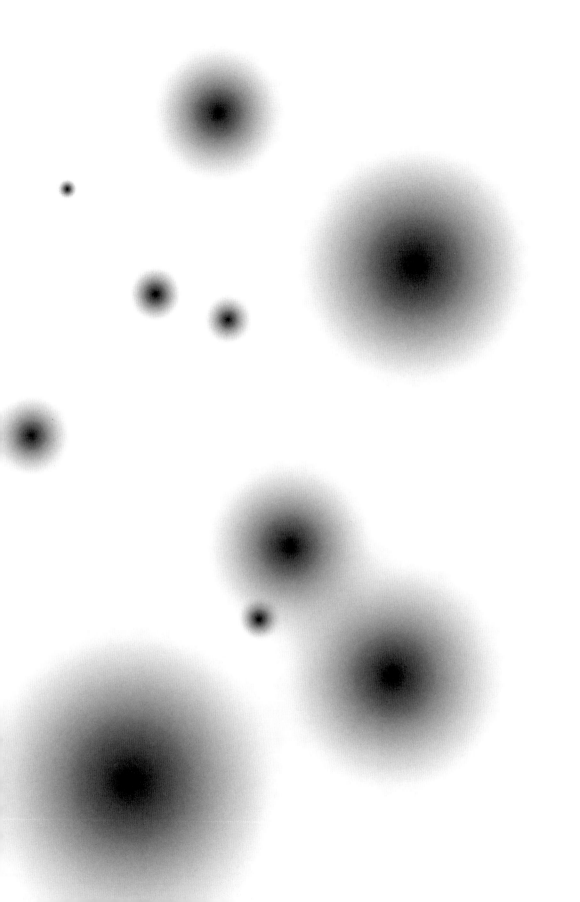

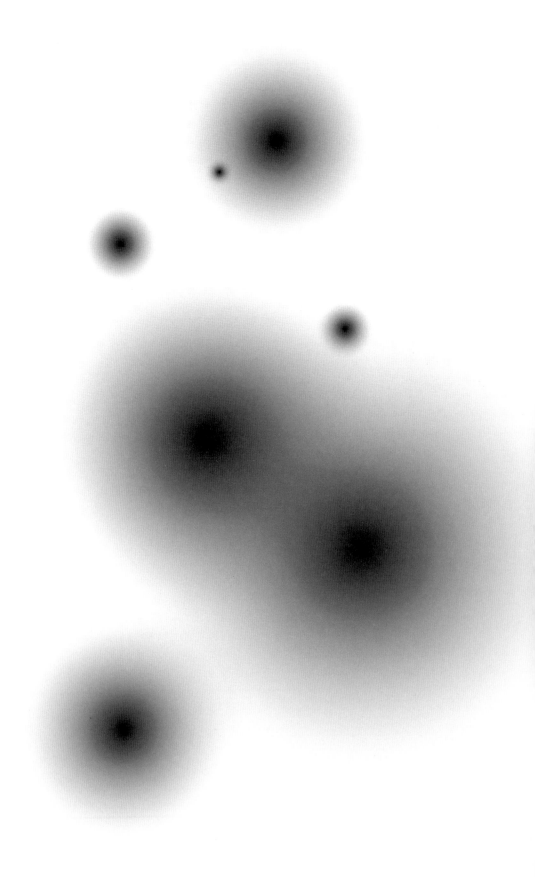

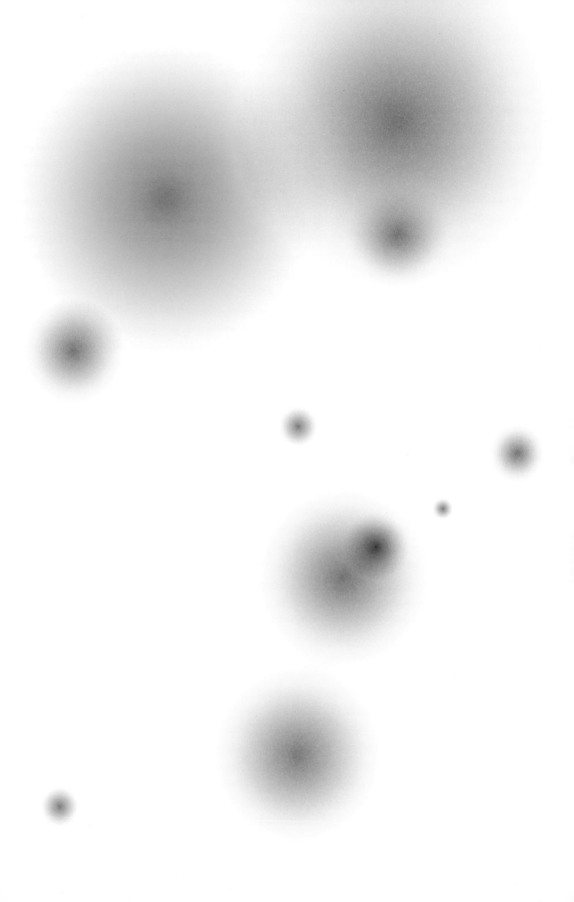

Jorinde Seijdel

The Subversive Effect of the Shadow Archive

On Florian Göttke's Toppled

Florian Göttke collected hundreds of press and amateur photographs of the toppling of statues of Saddam Hussein from the internet. He used this digital archive to create the iconographic project *Toppled*, as well as a special contribution to this issue of *Open*.[1] *Toppled* raises urgent questions about contemporary forms of iconoclasm and iconolatry, about the aesthetic and political effect of images in the contemporary public domain and about the potential of subversive shadow archives.

1. To get an impression of the project, not all of which is online, see http://www.Toppledsaddam.org/Toppled.html.

Statues and portraits of Saddam Hussein as general, demagogue, child-lover, Arab leader, devout Muslim, soldier, spiritual leader, businessman . . . Starting with the now iconic image of the toppling of the immense statue of Hussein with outstretched arm on Firdous Square in Baghdad on 9 April 2003, with the entry of the Americans, Florian Göttke's picture essay also follows the turbulent after-life of the statues of the deposed despot. Not only were they removed from their pedestals, they were also physically 'battered' afterwards by Iraqi citizens. American soldiers took photographs of each other posing in victory beside the remains. Pieces of the statues eventually ended up as war booty in American and English museums and are sold as souvenirs on internet auctions. Even before his arrest on 14 December 2003 and his hanging on 30 December 2006, the dictator became a zombie made of stone, bits and bytes.

Göttke's iconographic reading of the images that he gathered through systematic internet searches can be regarded as a special form of 'citizen journalism', but also as an inquiry into how images and representations are culturally determined. *Toppled* is a heterogeneous and hybrid archive in which amateur photographs and professional news images are juxtaposed in a non-hierarchical manner so as to create an informal report. It is a form of reporting arising from the mingling of different visual and media genres, political spheres and social domains and is thus far from unambiguous. A legion of narrative lines can be unravelled from it: for his contribution to this issue of *Open*, for example, Göttke followed the ways that American soldiers dealt with relics of the Saddam statues.

My concern here, however, is with the project as a whole. In the first place, *Toppled* addresses the problem of the phenomenon of iconoclasm, but it also takes a closer look at amateur photographs in relation to other snapshots by soldiers of the war in Iraq that fall outside the project. Finally, there is the question of how *Toppled* functions as a 'shadow archive'.

Iconoclash

The statues of Saddam gave expression to the carefully staged, excessive personality cult surrounding his person. Their removal from private and public spaces in Iraq was a special and in a certain sense impossible task. The iconoclastic urge to have done once and for all with the pictures and representations of a fallen ruler or a brought down power would seem to be vain in a visual, digital culture dominated by the logic of endless reproduction. Hardly any control, after all, can be exercised on the reproduction, distribution and circulation of images and symbols, nor on where and by whom they are seen and preserved.

The scenes of the toppling and destruction of the statues of Saddam immediately bring to mind other historical expressions of iconoclasm, whose 'victims' in modern times included Stalin, Hitler and Chiang Kai-shek. In the case of the recent iconoclasm in Iraq, however, it becomes particularly clear that our ability to witness it is by the grace of and through our passion for photographic images. Paradoxically, it is through the image that we experience iconoclasm. Images, products of our iconolatry and mania for images, endow the expressions of iconoclasm with maximum visibility. The destruction of images guarantees the production of images.

Images also become icons themselves – or idols, depending on one's point of view – that can be deployed as weapons in today's political, cultural and religious battlefields. To an increasing degree, wars also take place at the level of the image. The photograph of the toppling of the statue of Saddam on Firdous Square in Baghdad, for example, functions as an iconic image with regard to a particular phase of the war in Iraq and governs how it is represented and perceived. But at the same time it is doubtful whether an image that is itself an icon can indeed function as an objective representation of iconoclasm. Does not such an image always refer to itself rather than provide a view of reality?

In order to attain more insight into the complex relationship between icono-clasm, iconolatry, image and spectator, the French philosopher Bruno Latour introduced the notion of 'iconoclash'.[2] We can say there is an iconoclash between spectator and image when 'a profound and disturbing uncertainty exists concerning the role, power, status, danger and violence of an image or representation', says Latour. The iconic photograph of the iconoclasm directed against Saddam seems, then, to be a case of an intensified iconoclash operating at various levels: a 'clash' between (the status of) the photograph and what is depicted gives rise to iconoclashes between the viewer and the photographic image, as well as between the viewer and what is depicted. This must indeed have consequences for the public and political value of image and reality. What the image shows has happened, but the actual implications and intentions of image and event remain vague.

Decades ago, Jean Baudrillard described the image as the site of the disappear-ance of meaning, information and representation. After 9/11 he even wondered to what extent certain photographs have not become a parody of violence; it is no longer a question of the truth or falsity of images, but of their impact, which means that they have become an integral part of war. The image itself, as the vanishing point of reality, has become violent.[3]

Images and their effect and affect, can, however, also be judged more mildly; their violence is perhaps not purely nihilistic. Hal Foster's notion of 'traumatic realism' might offer a way out of the binary opposition that often dominates dis-course about reality and representation, between the image as referential or as Baudrillarian simulacrum. According to this notion, realistic documentary images can also be read as 'referential and simulacral, connected and disconnected, affec-

2. Bruno Latour, 'What is Icono-clash? Or is there a world beyond the image wars', in: Bruno Latour and Peter Weibel (eds.), *Iconoclash. Beyond the Image Wars in Science, Religion, and Art* (Cambridge, MA: MIT Press, 2002).

3. Jean Baudrillard, 'War Porn', in: *The Conspiracy of Art* (Cambridge, MA: Semiotext(e)/MIT Press, 2005), 205-210.

tive and affectless, critical and complacent'.[4] Precisely because these realistic images continue to appear time and time again and are repeated and widely distributed, they have the capacity to simultaneously protect us from, to reconcile ourselves with and to persuade us of a 'traumatic real'. Following Baudrillard, the iconoclasm, the trauma, in *Toppled* would lie more in the images themselves than in what they show; if we follow Foster, then this is the very reason that they form a buffer against the real.

4. Hal Foster, *The Return of the Real* (Cambridge, MA: MIT Press, 1996), 130. On this aspect see also Kari Anden-Papadopoulus, 'The Trauma of Representation. Visual Culture, Photojournalism and the September 11 Terrorist Attack', http://www.nordicom.gu.se/common/publ_pdf/32/32_089-104.pdf (accessed on 24 July 2007).

Disaster Tourism

The images from *Toppled* that Göttke selected for this issue of *Open* are amateur photographs taken by American soldiers during their mission in Iraq. The part of the *Toppled* archive that they belong to is called 'Appropriating Saddam', in which the Saddam statues or fragments of them function as objects to be photographed next to. The images reflect both a tourist attitude – 'I was there' – and expressions of superiority and the establishment of a new hierarchy: one of the photographs shows an American urinating against a remnant of a statue of Saddam, despite the sign prohibiting this.

As amateur photographs, disseminated and duplicated in the public realm via the internet, the soldiers' snapshots represent a new, emergent category of war pictures, to which the notorious photographs taken by American soldiers of Iraqi prisoners being tortured in the Abu Ghraib prison surely belong as well. These series of images, however, are similar in more ways: some of the Abu Ghraib photographs also feature the soldiers posing like tourists and appear to be intended for the home front or as souvenirs for later. The superior attitude whereby the 'foreign' or the 'other' – the Iraqi prisoners – is appropriated and to which they are subjected is fundamentally no different from the way the soldiers treat the statues.

It may not seem all that ethically correct to equate photographs of people being tortured with those of dismantled statues, and especially to make a comparison with tourist photographs. But studying and naming their shared formal and technical properties does reveal that they both emerge from a broader and egalitarian media and amusement culture. Susan Sontag pointed out that photographs of soldiers and their prisoners or war booty were formerly made as trophies to be preserved in the circumscribed space of a collection or photo album. Nowadays, says Sontag, such images are no longer 'objects' but messages to be disseminated and exchanged via the internet.[5]

5. Susan Sontag, 'Regarding the Torture of Others', *New York Times Magazine*, 23 May 2004.

The amateur photographs made by soldiers stem from popular media culture without really being able to detach themselves from it, even though what they show is so extreme or exceptional. A crucial question is how they subsequently function there, and then not at the level of representation, qua Baudrillard and the 'traumatic realism' of Foster, but at the level of their specific technical and medial definition.

Walter Benjamin proposed that the function of film and other modern media at the beginning of the last century was to teach people how to deal with the shock effects of urban modernity. Following on from this, the media theorist Richard Grusin suggests that the creation and distribution of digital images, similar to the photographs under discussion here, could be a way to disperse the shock or the traumatic affect of the war and the American presence in Iraq across media artefacts.[6] Taking the photos becomes an attempt to transfer the experience of the shock to a media memory. According to this argument, the formal and technical properties of digital photography and the internet are thus aids that enable us to cope with reality by delegating or deferring the sensation of it. The soldiers taking photographs or making films, therefore, are not appropriating reality, at least not directly, but are giving it away to an indefinite medial memory. There the images end up in an indefinable space in which every receiver/viewer is turned into a voyeur and accomplice. Just like the makers, however, they can always defer their responsibility or their involvement in the images by literally parting with them and circulating them further. In this sense, these image consumers are behaving in the same way as the soldiers/senders, that is, as an 'interpassive subject' who delegates his cognitive or perceptual occupation.[7] And by constantly rebounding the images from a personal to a public domain, they can never really be compromised.

6. Lecture by Richard Grusin, 'Affect, Mediality, and Abu Ghraib'. See http://www.unibg.it/dati/corsi/3025/13365-Abu%20Ghraib--Ljubljana-Bergamo2nda%20versione.pdf. For the illustrations: http://www.unibg.it/dati/corsi/3025/13399-Abu%20Ghraib--Bergamopowerpoint.pdf (accessed on 24 July 2007).

7. Slavoj Žižek, 'The Interpassive Subject', http://www.egs.edu/faculty/zizek/zizek-the-interpassive-subject.html (accessed on 24 July 2007).

Deepening of Iconic Memory

Are the realistic digital images, whether professional or amateur, and at the level both of representation (Foster) and their mediality (Grusin), aimed chiefly at minimalizing the traumatic effect of seeing or experiencing a shocking reality? Or has the image itself become iconoclastic (Baudrillard), resulting in a state of 'iconoclash'?

The subversive effect of *Toppled* as a shadow archive largely consists in its capacity to raise questions about images and their effect and about the way we deal with media today. It thus evokes new meanings and narratives, making revelations that relate critically to both the formal and informal sources from which it draws.

Toppled exhibits a narrative line that largely follows the chronology of the events. The captions remain close to what is depicted and are relatively straightforward and objective. But precisely because of this, space is created for the listener/viewer to arrive at interpretations of the images that are more analytical and

theoretical and that cause the linear narrative structure to disintegrate.

According to experimental psychology, 'iconic memory' is a type of short term visual memory that has a great capacity but is of very short duration: memory traces of visual impressions last about half a second before they decay. Iconic memory, understood here as a cultural metaphor for the fleeting way we deal with images nowadays, is reflected in *Toppled*, particularly because of the large amount of images (more than 400) and the speed with which they pass before us. At the same time, however, it is adjusted: the duration of the memory is extended through the concentration on a thematic selection and specific arrangement of pictures: they can thus be transferred, as it were, from a short-term to a long-time memory.

Now that the public domain is getting more and more clogged up with a morbid growth of images of uncertain origin and with unclear intentions, which are produced both by the conventional news media and the new informal media, parallel and experimental shadow archives like *Toppled* are of crucial importance. Not in order to bring us closer to the truth, but to guarantee forms and places of alternative publicity and signification. And to safeguard the image as a potential source of historical knowledge in both its aesthetic and political dimensions.

TEAM TCHM

Hollow Model

Art historian Kirsten Algera and designer Felix Janssens, of the design agency TEAM TCHM, have launched the project PRaudioGuide, in which they reflect on the 'hybrid city' and the role the mass media play in it. In connection with the radio documentary 'The Latest Buzz: In Search of Real Media', the editors of *Open* asked them to submit a contribution. *Hollow Model* features templates of the quasi-public in political communication.

political templates

Hollow Model

TEAM TCHM

IN THE MEDIA DEMOCRACY nowadays, waging politics is equivalent to interim management. Market research dictates political policy, participation models and media exposure legitimize the programme of electoral managers who 'mind the store' for four years. In this post-political environment, the public dimension has all but vanished; it is an instrument of communications strategy and is simulated in applause, chat sessions and 'treaties'. The contours of the public domain are barely visible, like a carcass; a template. 'Astroturf' is the American term for this simulation of public involvement, the instant variant of spontaneous 'grassroots' movements. At Schokland, or in Kyrgyzstan. Political scientist Gene Sharp is the international Astroturf Guru. Ever since the publication of his 'From Dictatorship to Democracy' in 1993, he has been considered the Clausowitz of non-violent warfare. Wherever he turns up, a 'Franchised Revolution' occurs in short order: orange, green or pink; tulip, rose or cedar. The script is expensive, but effective. This is democracy, and it costs a fortune.'

TEMPLATE 1: THE REVOLUTION

Expose your grassroots Hire Democracy

FRANCHISED REVOLUTIONS
after GENE SHARP

Bulldozer Revolution, Serbia 2000
Rose Revolution, Georgia 2003
Orange Revolution, Ukraine 2004
Cedar Revolution, Lebanon 2005
Tulip Revolution, Kyrgyzstan
2005

TEMPLATE 2: THE COMMUNICATIONS PLAN

Manage your citizens - Mediate their trust

1. From Problem to Challenge
..Subject.. represents an ever-increasing problem. And it is from this point of view that most people become and have become aware of the subject.

The individual experience of ..identifying several concrete, evocative examples.. dominates the perception of more and more people in regard to the ..subject.. Campaigns launched here and there are an initial attempt to involve the public – and over its heads, the political establishment – in the fact that ..subject.. is not only causing unpleasant experiences in ..for example, cities/motorways.., but is also fulfilling an essential role in meeting ..for example, daily needs.. Something self-evident to those who deal with the subject every day, an eye-opener for those who are merely, literally.. concrete example of the subject.. in a state of mind in which this concept is highly improbable. The high level of background knowledge among those directly involved entails the danger of skewed perspectives. Of the idea that the public does not want to be involved and perceives ..subject.. only as an inconvenience. This idea makes it tempting to restrict communications on the subject to a relatively small group of those directly involved and interested. With the risk that the communication of measures in this area ..cite examples.. (independently of a judgement about it) exude an atmosphere like the traditional 'official government announcement', which could and can count on little sympathy or attention.

From 'Framework for communications plan for Involvement and Bilateral Action – Compiled to facilitate the development of a service/network organization' HYPERLINK "http://www.zoutenpeper. nl/index.html"

TEMPLATE 3: THE TREATY

Legitimize your policy - Motivate through action

ENTERTAINMENT, POLITICS AND ORGANIZATIONAL MANAGE-MENT: THE HOLY TRINITY

Marco Borsato, Bert Koenders/ Elmer van Middelkoop, Lennart Booij (BKB) during the event 'Het akkoord van Schokland' (The Schokland Treaty) organized by the BKB agency, summer 2007.

HET AKKOORD

book reviews

Lex ter Braak, Gitta Luiten, Taco de Neef and Steven van Teeseling (eds.)
Second Opinion. Over beeldende kunstsubsidies in Nederland

NAi Publishers, Rotterdam, 2007, 128 pp., ISBN 978-90-5662-525-2, €17.50

Pascal Gielen

A collection of essays by the French sociologist of art Nathalie Heinich was translated into Dutch and published a few years ago, under the auspices of her special professorial chair, on behalf of the Boekman Foundation. It was not particularly in honour of the Dutch context that the book was given the title *Het Van Gogh-effect* (The Van Gogh Effect). At the time, Heinich had been obstinately hammering away for several years at a sociology of art that relies strongly on the 'Van Gogh model'.

Her more recent book, *L'élite artiste. Excellence et singularité en régime démocratique* (2005), uses much the same model. In reading *Second Opinion*, I was constantly reminded of the contents of *L'élite artiste*. Allow me to say a bit about it. The thesis that Heinich defends has it that Vincent van Gogh fulfils the function of a hinge between the academic system and modern art. What's more, even today his life and, in particular, his career represent the ideal model for an artist – the image of the artist who is almost completely unrecognized during his lifetime but goes on to enjoy the utmost fame long after death. In other words, a lack of rec-

ognition during an artist's life is supposed to guarantee his reputation as a great master in the future. According to Heinich, Van Gogh's legacy is an art world characterized by a singular regime in which uniqueness, authenticity and even excess are regarded as important values. Such a world is diametrically opposed to the dominant political model, democracy, which Heinrich says is not a singular but a collective regime with equality and anti-elitism as its core values. Thanks to its aristocratic heritage, the art world regularly conflicts with the political and social contexts in which it exists today. Because of his exceptional talent, says Heinich, the artist is, in fact, elitist.

Criticisms of the Dutch system of art subsidization expressed by various authors in *Second Opinion* fit easily into the tense relationship between the exceptional/aristocratic situation and the democratic regime of values. The present system is seen as being too democratic. Prevailing policies are not really conducive to artistic quality. Quality, after all, demands greater selectivity rather than consensual decisions by committees. On the other hand, one important

legitimation of the current system is that one cannot know today what the talent of the future is going to be. And so we 'let a thousand flowers bloom'. Such an argument can indeed be cited as a Van Gogh effect. What's worse, the Dutch subsidy system seems to be suffering from a genuine Van Gogh syndrome.

Perhaps it is indeed because of the art world's singular regime and elitism that there is so little debate. Public discussion is one of the more important democratic and thus non-aristocratic traditions. It is surprising that *Second Opinion* was not initiated by artists or other cultural actors. On the contrary, it is the director of The Netherlands Foundation for Visual Arts, Design and Architecture and the director of the Mondriaan Foundation – Lex ter Braak and Gitta Luiten, respectively – who have set the cat among the pigeons. This is not only peculiar but also courageous. It testifies at least to a proper degree of self-reflection. As becomes a good democracy, Ter Braak and Luiten conclude their book only after they have allowed a motley crowd – as colourful as the design of the book – of curators, gallery owners, museum directors, artists, academics and other interested parties to have their say. In their view, there are three lessons to be drawn from the discussion that they themselves have generated: a better balance should be found between subsidizing supply and demand, which in practice means more money for institutions; there should be higher subsidies for fewer artists, and therefore more selectivity in favour of excellent talent; and Dutch art should become more international.

Although I wholeheartedly endorse the conclusions, I cannot help but wonder whether they were predetermined by the initiators. In the book I recognize both supporters and opponents, to be sure, although the latter are noticeably in the minority. Only one or two, for example, dare to state that the Dutch subsidy system is not bad at all, that Dutch artists are often to be seen abroad, or that the quality of their work is actually very good. They also contradict and at the same time put into perspective the jeering quip one sometimes hears abroad about the artist who is 'world famous, but then only in Holland'. *Second Opinion* unfortunately lacks any empirical data that would support or deny such a theory, unless we regard *Elsevier*'s top hundred artists as scientific evidence. No, *Second Opinion* remains a book of opinions, many of which regularly overlap and, in a few cases, contradict one another. The reader all too quickly ends up in a game of 'tis not! 'tis so! Who is in the right and has good reasons for being so?

Indeed, a democracy asks for a debate before decisions are taken, and such a debate is conducted, or at least staged, in *Second Opinion*. It remains to be seen what the next steps will be. After the proffering of motley opinions, it is time to make clear, well-grounded choices. That's why this book needs a sequel, a thorough study about the real impact of the Dutch subsidy system, preferably in comparison with a few other countries. Then the question can be posed as to what position Dutch art wants to assume within the global art world. Does it want to internationalize simply so that it can run with the fleeting global trends in art? Or should it aim at an identity of its own, with its own accents that are deemed of value from a cultural and artistic point of view? Do we want an Amsterdam version of Guggenheim Bilbao, or is the Serralves Museum in Porto a better model? Do we want artists who quickly make their mark in the international media and just as quickly burn out, or do we want them to develop lasting international careers? Do we want an art world that sails the globe or one that is anchored in the 'glocal'? In other words, a policy that invests more in institutions, deals more selectively with subsidies to artists and internationalizes in a better way can leave plenty of room for manoeuvring. Only when a clear view of such matters has been developed can we look forward to a vigorous 'First Decision'.

Ned Rossiter
Organized Networks: Media Theory, Creative Labour, New Institutions,

Eric Kluitenberg

NAi Publishers, Rotterdam, in association with the Institute of Network Cultures, Hogeschool van Amsterdam, 2006, ISBN 978-90-5662-526-9, € 19.50

During the New Network Theory Conference organized by the University of Amsterdam and the Hogeschool van Amsterdam in late June 2007, the question of just what was meant by the term 'network' came up several times, and with good reason. After all, virtually all social relations are network relations. What was meant in this case were technologically facilitated and media networks, which have undergone a boom as electronic agorae as a result of the explosive growth of the internet.

While the evolution of the internet is subject to the influences of countless strategic interests, the 'network of networks' is still associated with a certain level of disorder and lack of control. Thus the need to define and delineate the term 'network' becomes all the more urgent when an entire book is devoted to 'organized networks'. This raises many questions, for did 'we' (as average internet users) not wish *not* to have to deal with all these strategic interests? Was not the very potential of the internet that it could bring together large groups of people with shared interests, without having to organize them beforehand? Was not the charm of the internet in fact the 'unorganized network'?

These questions have not escaped the notice of Ned Rossiter, who teaches media studies at the University of Ulster

and is a research fellow at the Centre for Cultural Research at the University of Western Sydney. They are the premise of his extensive research. He wonders how these 'unorganized networks' maintain themselves. Who actually undertakes the necessary work, and under what conditions? Are there institutional structures that support the new internet-related networks? If so, which ones and, more importantly, why? Are new institutional connections and new forms of social organization being created? Are new forms not urgently needed?

For some time, an information or network economy has reigned alongside the elusive, spontaneous and bottom-up organized networks, partly a product of the service economy (which is based, after all, largely on processing information and which far outpaces, in terms of size, the primary production sectors in every advanced industrial country) and partly of the creative industry. The digitization of the design process and the importance of design in virtually all applications of information have made the creative industry the spearhead of today's economic development. It is a young, dynamic sector in which the informal relations (the quasi-'unorganized' relations) of the internet are elevated to the level of an all-encompassing operational culture. Rossiter is

not the first to pose the question of what this means in concrete terms for labour relations within the creative industry. Andrew Ross, for instance, wrote a fine book entitled *No Collar* on relations within the 'informal workplace', and the Italian sociologist Maurizio Lazzarato dubbed the new forms of labour in the information society *lavoro immateriale* (immaterial labour). From very divergent backgrounds, Ross, Lazzarato and Rossiter take uncommonly sceptical and critical positions towards these new 'immaterial' labour relations and the disappearance of traditional labour relations, along with the guarantees and the protection of rights and responsibilities that the old workplace entailed.

Rossiter points out that the primary function of a creative-industry worker is to create intellectual property (IP). This involves the direct commercial turnover of marketable ideas and their forms (image, sound, design, experiences), which is fundamentally different from the reputation-based economics of the traditional art world, in which incomes are generated indirectly by building up a reputation that leads to higher valuation for works and services. The privatization of cultural production, with its obsessive control over and protection of intellectual property (witness the hysterical discussions in the music industry), is the most significant hallmark of the creative industry. It represents a serious threat to the cultural public domain.

In Rossiter's view, something similar is taking place in the social and political public domain. Representative democracy seems to be transforming definitively into what he calls, in a paraphrase, a 'shareholder democracy'. Are we becoming, instead of citizens in a civil democracy, shareholders in a fully privatized society? A society in which we, as 'investors' in this society, receive a return on investment (ROI) of maximum efficiency from our collective institutions, under penalty of dismissal for executive boards in the case of policy failures, hostile mergers, takeovers, or divestitures – led by activist 'shareholders'.

In Rossiter's book, the 'state' seems to have turned into an anachronism: a few condescending words are occasionally expended on this mastodon, but mostly to emphasize how hopelessly obsolete and completely irrelevant the institution has become. The growing supranational social structure, in which corporations and conglomerates as well as NGOs and citizens' movements operate at an international level, has led to entirely new economic and sociopolitical power relations. This raises the question of whether there are new institutional structures capable of taking over the role of old social institutions (the state, trade unions) under these altered conditions. New embodiments of such institutions are crucial if society is to be kept from turning into a fully liberalized jungle in which the only law is that of the fittest.

Rossiter sees prototypes emerging in various places, such as the World Summit on the Information Society. This virtually global initiative by NGO-type organizations experiments in exemplary fashion with new forms of management and policy for the information society. To Rossiter, it is the initiative's process-based character that is particularly remarkable. He identifies in it the outlines of a new type of 'processual democracy' that is no longer based on the principle of representation but is, instead, the product of constant interaction among diverse interest groups and social actors in a real-time networked context.

These new forms of process regulation give rise to new organized networks that are more structured and more durable than the informal networks of the internet's early phase of development. They form the backbone of the new supranational civil movements that are gradually taking over the role of traditional social institutions, focusing on working conditions, education, healthcare, the environment, minority rights and so forth.

It is a good thing that – in the face of the reigning euphoria about the internet as a free space, the cultivation of the creative industry, the informal (no-collar) workplace, the hysteria surrounding user-generated content and Web 2.0 – Rossiter is raising serious questions about accountability, political operating space and issues such as labour relations, authority, income and the need for new institutional forms in the network society. In placing such a major emphasis on the political dimensions of these developments and on their material and labour-related conditions, however, he ignores the highly non-utilitarian and sometimes apparently nihilist character of 90 per cent or more of internet traffic and use. It is as though the ostensibly aimless experience of the great overwhelming majority of internet users and their cultures of use are of no interest to Rossiter. In a kind of neo-Gramscian move, they are relegated to the sidelines as by-products of subordinate importance and, at best, an illusory deception of the de facto oppressed masses. If this is genuinely the underlying, implicit assumption on which Rossiter based his book (he is not clear about this), he has grossly underestimated the 'sovereign' network subject.

Three Blogs Devoted to
Contemporary Art

Arie Altena

http://www.ctrlaltdelete.org
http://www.we-make-money-not-art.com
http://www.trendbeheer.com

Even people who blog journalistically – with a view to producing information and reportage for a group of readers – do so first and foremost for themselves. The American political philosopher Jodi Dean recently characterized blogging as 'a practice for managing the self under the conditions of communicative capitalism'.[1]

Blogging has more to do with the design and presentation (performance) of the blogger's (public) self than with journalism or the production of a publication in the classic sense. You can see it as a form of personal online information-processing and reflection – even though such reflection may consist of no more than the choice of a couple of photos. That it provokes reactions, that an audience may (sometimes) form around a blog, is of secondary importance. Of course, certain blogs put an emphasis on debate, host heated and/or substantive discussions, and raise and invite comment on ideas, but generally speaking these blogs are a minority. And although it's true that a loose sense of community takes shape in links between various blogs, and in the fact that they react to one another, such communities seldom take to the streets or manage to turn their concerns into public issues. The possibility should not be entirely ruled out, however. It happens more often in non-Western countries, where blogs and other

DIY online publications are the only form of alternative journalism. The fact is that most bloggers write for themselves. They don't have a public; they have readers.

Take Peter Luining, Net artist and 'internetter' from day one. On his weblog he documents things that have struck him on his walks around Amsterdam. The walks began as a way of shedding the excess weight accumulated during more than ten years of internet use. (It would be hard to imagine a nicer example of the proposition that blogging helps to keep you healthy in the presence of all that media excess.) In reporting on exhibitions he has visited, he includes photographs and impressions. Recurrent elements provide the appeal ('stickyness') of Luining's art log, such as art spotted on eBay or among rubbish on the street ('Art is lying on the street'). Although it is possible to infer a view of art from Luining's choices, he refrains from explicit criticism on his blog. This is a deliberate policy. Criticism means proffering considered arguments, making a substantiated 'distinction between', and doing so takes time. As long as you don't offer criticism you can safely follow your own inclinations; you can get away with ignoring important matters and paying attention to trivia. Hence the 'lightness' of many blogs, which can be seen as a positive quality. Those who indulge in

unsupported, decontextualized criticism in public very soon descend into indiscriminate ranting, ridiculing or blowing their own trumpets. Which is why Luining and other bloggers who prefer not to be seen as loudmouths or self-promoters are clever enough to let the chosen material speak for itself. It is up to us to draw conclusions.

The blog we-make-money-not-art.com has developed into a source of news and commentary from the new media scene, thanks to the approach adopted by Regine Debatty, who is a journalist, not an artist. Debatty writes long pieces, publishes interviews, and visits the latest media festivals and exhibitions. She pursues her own interests but uses her journalistic experience to produce a readable and interesting publication. To safeguard her position and professionalism, she takes a balanced approach, resulting in a much more explicit view of media art than a blunt expression of her opinions would have produced. Debatty establishes links between art and current technological, between social and scientific developments, and builds bridges to design, consumer electronics, games and internet culture. From the perspective of art criticism, it is significant that Debatty doesn't start from the history of the avant-garde or the tradition of European media criticism. On the contrary, she has a positive view of art: art is the creation of experiences, is about making discoveries; it opens the way for discovery and, yes, also asks questions.

It has been claimed, especially since 2001, that blogs are an invitation to engage in conversation. Blog software makers promote blogging as a way to 'publish your ideas, get feedback!' This claim does not apply to the art blogs mentioned here: Luining does not invite reader reactions, and although Debatty does, her invitation seldom leads to discussion. In terms of graphic design, format and technology, the Dutch art blog Trendbeheer (Jeroen Bosch, Marc Bijl, Niels Post, Hans van der Riet and Jaap Verhoeven), belongs to the genre of blogs that have emerged since 2003 and which feature comments, automatic insertion of 'delicious links', tags and an overview of the latest reactions. Turnover is high, with several contributions a day. Or, as the American blog ideology of the top 100 Bloggers stipulates: publish a lot and often in order to create a readership and keep readers happy. Compared with those of Luining and Debatty, entries in this genre are more sarcastic, funnier and more provocative. There is occasional harassment, leading to a spate of reactions nearly always from the same people: those who make nuanced remarks and others who are a pain in the ass. Trendbeheer's sometimes satirical, I-don't-give-a-damn-about-anything tone is adept at deflating hypes and misplaced pomposity. In that sense, Trendbeheer appears to be more critical than Luining and even Debatty. But ultimately it doesn't go beyond mockery; it never rises to the level of polemics, let alone criticism.

Actually, Trendbeheer has no desire to engage in art criticism or to conduct a theoretical debate on art. In saying this, I do not mean to denigrate the quality of the information and links on offer but simply to comment on the tone of the blog. Those who don't care for it or can't stand it are welcome to look elsewhere. After all, given the wealth of information on the internet and the possibility of doing a better job yourself, why would you spend a lot of time criticizing the blinkered vision of one particular blog?

Anyone who concludes from my remarks that blogs excel at registering and commenting on things and fall short when it comes to reviewing and criticizing – in other words, fall short in creating a public sphere – is too hung up on a classic notion of the function of the press. Such a conclusion misses the implicit view of art that gradually develops on a blog, the connections that are made, the presence of many perspectives, and the networks that readers can scour. A blog is permanently 'under construction'; entries are temporal – and all that temporality is archived. There is a sense of a vision that is continually being formed – that is examined and interrogated but seldom explicitly defined. To be able 'understand' what is happening, a reader needs to follow a blog for a while (or to read three months' worth of reports in one go). Over time, a blog's lightness may start to acquire more gravitas.

1. See Jodi Dean, 'I cite, "Liquid Modernity"', 30 May 2007, http://jdeanicite.typepad.com/ i_cite/2007/05/liquid_modernit. html

Joke Brouwer and Arjen Mulder (eds.)
Interact or Die!

Omar Muñoz Cremers

NAi Publishers and V2_, Institute for the Unstable Media,
ISBN 978-90-5662-577-1
(English edition), € 22.50

Interact or Die! is a collection of essays published to accompany the Dutch Electronic Art Festival 2007, held in Rotterdam from 10 to 20 April. At first sight, the book looks like a conventional catalogue, with interactive works of art shown during the festival neutrally described in various sections throughout the book, including good and intriguing work by, among others, Workspace Unlimited, Exonemo and Herwig Weiser. The hilarious and inimitable project *Amazon Noir: The Big Book Crime* by Alessandro Ludovico and Paolo Circio of Übermorgen shows that interactive art is going through a fertile and multifaceted period. But anyone looking for a general theory about interactive art will be disappointed. Hurtling along with the texts and images is a stream of ideas dealing loosely with the theme of interactivity in an attempt to evoke associations with the works of art. Joke Brouwer and Arjen Mulder write in their foreword that 'interaction is a defining characteristic of every living being' and go on to state that '*Interact or Die!* is about the way in which random behaviour in networks creates strong but flexible structures and forms, without there being a central designing coordinator or code that pushes the process into a definitive direction or form. It explores how interaction both forms and selects the effective, functioning parts of networks and leaves the nonef-

fective parts to die.' This description is abstract enough to apply to a multitude of areas. In 'The Exercise of Interactive Art' Mulder provides a survey and a vigorous analysis of interactive art, using examples by Lygia Clark and Felix Gonzalez-Torres to define an art that changes through the agency of the spectator. As an object, the artwork itself is nothing and can even be destroyed in the process of interaction or acquisition of meaning. According to Mulder, interactive art has a number of implications for the relationships between artist and consumer and between gallery and public space, as well as for the experience of the spectator who realizes that 'self' is a product of interaction with other persons and objects. It reflects a continuous process of change whose effect extends to the global level. Mulder's argument that interactive art is the art of the moment (as both a process of realization and of 'where it is happening in art', it is the art of the age of globalization) is subtly contradicted, however, by Brian Massumi. In his view, interactivity has a tyrannical side, and its relationship with power is not neutral. The most effective and 'loving' power mechanisms are often capable of binding subjects by giving them the opportunity to express themselves. With this warning at the back of one's mind, he says, it is necessary to evaluate interactivity critically: which experiences produce in-

teractivity, which forms of life are able to develop such experiences, and what sort of power regimes are thus created? Massumi makes a distinction between art that focuses on an explicit political content and art that seeks dynamic forms and leads to an open process of discovery.

The rest of *Interact or Die!* deals much less, if at all, with interactive art, although this hardly detracts from its readability. Essays emanating from the fields of biology and architecture in particular show that these disciplines are thriving. Sean B. Carroll begins by explaining how interactivity works in 'evo devo' (evolutionary development biology), a new branch of biology that examines the area between development (how an individual creature is constructed) and evolution (how the diversity of creatures changes). The interview with Carroll contains information that most lay persons will find quite technical and detailed, but he also offers intriguing insights into the common toolbox of genes, for example, that determines the physique of most animals.

One of the stronger aspects of the book is the juxtaposition of two very different ideas on biology. Just when you've been convinced by Carroll, Eva Jablonka adds her comments about four-dimensional evolution and epigenetic inheritance. She is a pliant thinker, which may help explain why, under the influence of molecular biology's lack of dogmatism, the field is so on the go at the moment. The discussion ultimately leads to interesting speculations on the evolution of the capacity for language, whereby culture acquires a more dynamic place in biology.

The influence of biology on architecture becomes clear in the interview with Detlef Mertins, who makes it all too clear that architects are the last idealists. Under the self-coined term 'bioconstructivism', Mertins is working on an alternative history of architecture inspired by biology. Mertins also succeeds in linking interactivity, in the sense of people living in relation to architecture, with the enthusiasm for the new and the unknown evinced by the architecture of the 1920s, '50s and '60s: 'Architecture was intended to open the way for and support experiments in future paradigms of living.'

Enough interesting paths for further thought, but after reading *Interact or Die!* one is left with a latent feeling of discomfort about the 'state of thinking', the status of the intellectual. Ultimately, this sort of rhizomatous book is disorientating, mainly because the reader is unable to shake the impression that the majority of contributions are hardly more than personal obsessions. At the same time, of course, no exceptional new ideas, such as those of Jablonka, are created without obsession. Some disciplines, however, are better at channelling these than others. Philosophy in particular feels deficient at the moment and finds it hard to escape a certain stasis, a lack of future-directed ideas. Thus we can see it as an omen that people are turning for inspiration to forgotten thinkers, the last gold lodes preceding the postmodern rupture, as exemplified by Gilbert Simondon, whose contribution concludes the book.

ABOUT THE CONTRIBUTORS

Arie Altena (NL) writes about art, technology and new media. He is an editor/researcher at the V2_Archief in Rotterdam, teaches Interactive Media and Environments at the Frank Mohr Institute and is a co-organizer of Sonic Acts. In 2006 he conducted research at the Jan van Eyck Academie. His blog research project, *In the Loop*, is part of the *Ubiscribe* project, for which he also edited the POD book *Pervasive Personal Participatory, Ubiscribe 0.9.0* (2006).

Dr. Albert Benschop (NL) was a lecturer and researcher at the Universiteit van Amsterdam for many years. He is the founder of the world's most consulted social-science information system, SocioSite (www.sociosite.net), and founding father of net sociology in the Netherlands (www.sociosite.org).

Irene Costera Meijer (NL) is a senior lecturer in television and popular culture in the Media & Culture department at the Universiteit van Amsterdam. She has written a large number of articles on the quality of television. Her book *De toekomst van het nieuws* was published in 2006. As a researcher she frequently holds workshops for journalists and programme makers working for broadcast organizations and daily newspapers.

David Garcia (GB) is a writer, artist and professor of Design for Digital Culture at the University of Portsmouth and the Utrecht School of the Arts. He makes installations, videos and television programmes and writes about new media and internet culture. He was one of the people behind The Next 5 Minutes (1994-2003), a series of international conferences and exhibition on electronic communications and new social movements. He is currently involved in (Un)common Ground, a series of events and publications on this topic.

Pascal Gielen (BE) teaches art sociology and policy at the University of Groningen and holds the lectureship of the Practice of Art in Society at the Fontys University of Fine and Performing Arts in Tilburg. He is the author of such books as *Esthetica voor Beslissers* (2001), *Kunst in Netwerken* (2003) and (with Rudi Laermans) *Een omgeving voor Actuele Kunst* (2004) and *Cultureel Goed* (2005). His latest book is entitled *De Onbereikbare Binnenkant van het Verleden* (2007).

Florian Göttke (G) is a visual artist based in Amsterdam. His work is regularly exhibited throughout the Netherlands and abroad. www.floriangoettke.com

Richard Grusin (USA) is a professor and chair of the English Department at Wayne State University. His books include *Remediation: Understanding New Media* (1999) with Jay David Bolter. He is currently working on the book *Premediation: Affect, Mediality in America after 9/11* (working title).

Henry Jenkins (USA) is the Director of the MIT Comparative Media Studies Program. His newest books include *Convergence Culture: Where Old and New Media Collide* and *Fans, Bloggers and Gamers: Exploring Participatory Culture*. www.henryjenkins.org.

Dingeman Kuilman (NL) is director of Premsela Dutch Platform for Design and Fashion, based in Amsterdam.

Geert Lovink (NL) is a Dutch-Australian media theorist and internet critic and is a lecturer at the Hogeschool van Amsterdam, where he has led the Institute for Network Culture since 2004. Aside from launching such projects as nettime and fibreculture, he is the author of *Dark Fiber* (2002), *Uncanny Networks* (2004) and *My First Recession*. His book *Zero Comments, Blogging and Critical Internet Culture* (2007) was recently published.

Eric Kluitenberg (NL), as an independent writer, theorist and organizer, focuses on themes involving culture, media and technology. He has compiled such publications as *Het Boek van de imaginaire media* (2006) and *Open* no. 11, 'Hybrid Space' (as guest editor). He also coordinates the media programme at De Balie, in Amsterdam.

Bert Kommerij (NL) works at the RVU broadcast organization in Hilversum. He specializes in fiction. He writes and directs radio plays, does voice-overs for radio and television programmes, is a photographer and develops internet projects on his 'worklog': www.nieuwe-verhalen.blogspot.com.

Oliver Marchart (Aus) teaches in the Sociology department at the University of Lucerne. His recent books include *Post-foundational Political Thought: Political Difference in Nancy, Lefort, Badiou and Laclau* (2007), *Neu beginnen. Hannah Arendt, die Revolution und die Globalisierung* (2005). *Ästhetik des Öffentlichen. Eine politische Theorie künstlerischer Praxis* (2008) is due to be published shortly.

Omar Muñoz Cremers (NL) is a cultural sociologist and writer. His essays have previously been published in *Mediamatic*, *De Gids*, *Multitudes* and *Metropolis M*. His first novel is entitled *Droomstof* (2007). He lives and works in Amsterdam.

Maarten Reesink NL) has been affiliated since 1993 with the Media & Culture (formerly Film and Television Studies) Chair Group at the Universiteit van Amsterdam, where he was involved in the development of the television studies specialization. His own specializations are reality television and infotainment.

TEAM TCHM (NL) develops strategies, designs information and organizes communications. TEAM TCHM is currently reviewing its operating practice.

Martijn de Waal (NL) is affiliated as a researcher with the practical philosophy section at the University of Groningen and with the Media Studies section at the Universiteit van Amsterdam. He is also a freelance writer and consultant to such organizations as the Dutch Cultural Broadcasting Fund and the Mondriaan Foundation. He is the co-founder of DeNieuwe-Reporter.nl – a professional group weblog on technology, journalism, media and society. His research themes are new media, the public sphere and urban culture.

Willem van Weelden (NL) teaches at the Rietveld Academie in Amsterdam and the Sint-Lucas Academie in Brussels. He is also an independent researcher and writer in the field of new media, art and design.

Geert van de Wetering (NL) is a journalist and programme maker. He worked for six years for VPRO Television, where he was the creator and producer of such programmes as *Nachtpodium* and *Picabia*. He has also written for the *De Volkskrant* newsaper and many magazines. He currently works as a freelance journalist and director.

CREDITS

Open Cahier on Art and the Public
Domain. Volume 6 (2007) no. 13

Editors Jorinde Seijdel
(editor in chief), Liesbeth Melis
(final editing)

English copy editor D'Laine Camp
Dutch-English translations Pierre
Bouvier (editorial, interview
with Bas Könning, text 'Hot
Spot' by Geert van de Wetering,
text by Irene Costera Meijer and
Maarten Reesink, book review by
Eric Kluitenberg); Michael Gibbs
(interview with Richard Rogers,
text by Jorinde Seijdel, book
review by Pascal Gielen); Robyn de
Jong-Dalziel (text by Martijn de
Waal, column by Dingeman Kuilman,
book review by Arie Altena); Wendy
van Os (text by Bert Kommerij);
Connie Menting (text by Albert
Benschop)

Graphic design Thomas Buxó and
Klaartje van Eijk, Amsterdam
Printing and lithography Die Keure,
Brugge
Project coordinator Marieke van
Giersbergen, NAi Publishers
Publisher Eelco van Welie,
NAi Publishers

Open is published twice a year
Open 14 will be published in May
2008

Editorial address

SKOR
Ruysdaelkade 2
1072 AG Amsterdam
the Netherlands
Tel +31 (0)20 6722525
Fax +31 (0)20 3792809
open@skor.nl
www.opencahier.nl

SUBSCRIPTIONS

Abonnementenland
Postbus 20
1910 AA Uitgeest
the Netherlands
0900 - ABOLAND (0900 – 2265263,
€ 0,10 per minute)
Fax +31 (0)251 310405
www.aboland.nl.

PRICE PER ISSUE

€ 28.50

SUBSCRIPRION PRICES

(postage included)
the Netherlands: € 39,50
Within Europe: € 49.00
Outside Europe: € 55.00
Students: € 29.50

SUBSCRIPTION CANCELLATION

Cancellations (in writing only)
must be received by Abonnementenland eight weeks prior to the
end of the subscription period.
Subscriptions not cancelled in
time are automatically renewed
for one year.

For works of visual artists affiliated with a CISAC-organization
the copyrights have been settled with Beeldrecht in Amsterdam.
© 2007, c/o Beeldrecht Amsterdam

NAi Publishers is an internationally orientated publisher
specialized in developing, producing and distributing books on
architecture, visual arts and related disciplines.
www.naipublishers.nl info@naipublishers.nl

It was not possible to find all the copyright holders of the
illustrations used. Interested parties are requested to contact
NAi Publishers, Mauritsweg 23, 3012 JR Rotterdam, The Netherlands.

Available in North, South and Central America through D.A.P./
Distributed Art Publishers Inc, 155 Sixth Avenue 2nd Floor, New
York, NY 10013-1507, Tel 212 6271999, Fax 212 6279484.

Available in the United Kingdom and Ireland through Art Data,
12 Bell Industrial Estate, 50 Cunnington Street, London W4 5HB,
Tel 208 7471061, Fax 208 7422319.

Printed and bound in Belgium

ISSN 1570-4181
ISBN 978-90-5662-604-4

open

*For a comprehensive overview of contents according to author,
article and theme, see www.opencahier.nl*

(IN)SECURITY

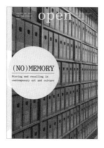

(NO)MEMORY

(IN)VISIBILITY

SOUND

(IN)TOLERANCE

HYBRID SPACE

FREEDOM OF
CULTURE